BORNE BY THE RIVER

*Canoeing the Delaware from
Headwaters to Home*

RICK VAN NOY

THREE HILLS

AN IMPRINT OF CORNELL UNIVERSITY PRESS

ITHACA AND LONDON

First published 2024 by Cornell University Press
Printed in the United States of America

Library of Congress Cataloging-in-Publication Data

Names: Van Noy, Rick, 1966– author.
Title: Borne by the river : canoeing the Delaware from headwaters to home / Rick Van Noy.
Other titles: Canoeing the Delaware from headwaters to home
Description: Ithaca : Three Hills, an imprint of Cornell University Press, 2024. | Includes
    bibliographical references.
Identifiers: LCCN 2023045582 (print) | LCCN 2023045583 (ebook) |
    ISBN 9781501775116 (paperback) | ISBN 9781501775130 (epub) |
    ISBN 9781501775123 (pdf)
Subjects: LCSH: Canoes and canoeing—Delaware River (N.Y.-Del. and N.J.) |
    Delaware River (N.Y.-Del. and N.J.)—Description and travel. |
    Delaware River (N.Y.-Del. and N.J.)—History.
Classification: LCC F157.D4 V36 2024 (print) | LCC F157.D4 (ebook) |
    DDC 917.49—dc23/eng/20231010
LC record available at https://lccn.loc.gov/2023045582
LC ebook record available at https://lccn.loc.gov/2023045583

BORNE BY THE RIVER

For my mother, Elene

I was born upon thy banks, River,
My blood flows in thy stream,
And thou meanderest forever
At the bottom of my dream.
Henry David Thoreau

CONTENTS

BRIDGES

When traveling downriver, no signs tell you where you are, which can be part of the appeal. Bridges are among the best means to wayfinding on a river, and they also signify towns to rest or resupply. There are some fifty of them from Hancock to the bay, many of historic and architectural significance. I have included pictures of ten here, for those marking the beginning, end, and each day in the journey. The images should give some indication of the width and characteristics of the river, the weather and mood of each segment, bridge by bridge.

Hancock, New York—begin
Lordville-Equinunk—day 2
Narrowsburg-Darbytown—day 3
Barryville-Shohola—day 4
Milford-Montague—day 5

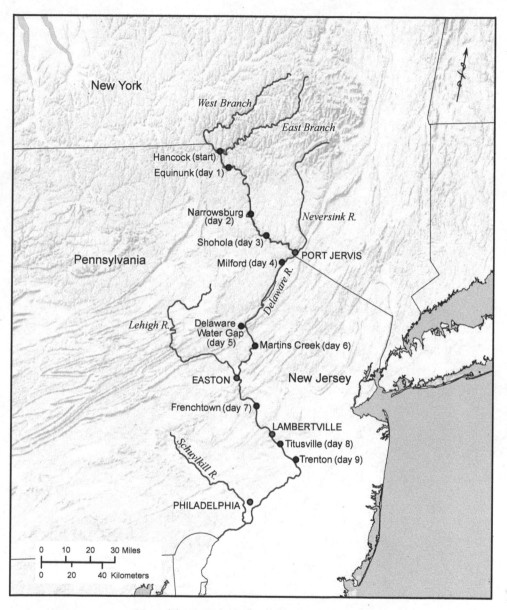

Map of the watershed, Hancock to Delaware Bay.

HEADWATERS

All stories have beginnings. Rivers do too. The beginnings of this river are hard to trace, though the main stem of the Delaware starts here in Hancock, New York, where the East and West Branches unite. But before those, there are creeks, and springs, and tiny rivulets. Some snowmelt from the Catskill and Pocono Mountains, runoff from farms, the rain falling off the tin roof of an old barn, sliding off pitched eaves—it all ends up here, in this river.

Where it provides drinking water for some fifteen million people, including the residents of New York City and Philadelphia, and is the longest undammed river in the East. I begin at mile 330 and have 200 miles between me and Trenton, where the river turns tidal, estuarial. Were I to navigate those currents, and dodge transport ships, another 130 miles would get me to Cape May and the Delaware Bay.

In 1609 Henry Hudson sailed the *Halve Maen* (half-moon) into the bay and what he called the South River, claiming it for Holland and the Dutch East India Company. Dutch settler Adriaen van der Donck would write in midcentury that it was among "the most beautiful, best, and pleasantest rivers in the world." Hudson and early Dutch settlers likely saw Natives in canoes who already had a claim to it. They called it Lenape Whittuck, "river of the Lenape," or Lenape Sipu. The Dutch called it Viskill, "great fish river." Delaware comes from Thomas West, the Baron de la Warr, the first governor of Jamestown, who never actually saw the bay, river, or people that would bear his name.

Once seriously impaired, from the 1900s to the 1972 Clean Water Act, the health of the river is widely hailed as an environmental success story, earning 2020 "river of the year" honors from the organization American Rivers. Two-thirds of my trip is through a Wild and Scenic River, a federal designation intended to safeguard the "outstandingly remarkable" values of a river (less than 1 percent of US rivers have this designation), but this river will not feel that wild. In fact, part of what intrigues me about it is the way it interlaces with history, slices through river towns, including this one, Hancock, but also Port Jervis, Dingman's Ferry, Easton, Upper Black Eddy, Frenchtown, Stockton, Lambertville, New Hope.

A writer of both ponds and rivers, Henry David Thoreau wrote in his journal (July 2, 1858) that rivers had more of a "liberating influence" than lakes, leading our eyes and thoughts to the sea, to ports near and far, transporting us in body and spirit. "A river touching the back of a town is like a wing, it may be unused as yet, but ready to waft it over the world. With its rapid current it is a slightly fluttering wing. River towns are winged towns."

These towns grew up along the river because the river provided a kind of highway, and our civilization's first footsteps, paths, and roads were often guided by rivers. A river runs through the first written story circa 1800 BC, pieced together through fragmentary tablets. King Gilgamesh and his companion Enkidu unleash the wrath of the gods when they cut down trees from a sacred forest and float them downriver, resulting in Enkidu's death. Gilgamesh sails to the underworld to search for immortality, meets a Noah-like survivor of a river flood, but returns empty-handed. Upon his death, the people of Uruk divert the Euphrates and bury the king so that once the river resumes its normal course it flows over the dead king's grave. Time, and rivers, can't be beaten. Or they are kings and spirits themselves.

In the Bible, a river flowed out of Eden to water the garden, then divided into four branches. *Shall we gather at the river?* the song asks. *Take me to the river*, sing the Talking Heads (via Al Green). Jersey's Boss sings about going down to the river to dive, to wash away the despair.

Rivers carry people and goods but also meaning. And this one means something to me.

My own story starts in the city where I will end. I was born in Trenton and grew up in one of those winged towns, Titusville. It's just upstream from the site of Washington's historic crossing, which imbued the place with more significance, more meaning.

I worked summers at a marina and canoe outfitter. People would rent canoes and take them upstream, or I would drive them. On a wall near the register were listed the towns and their mileages, and we had maps. From the Delaware River Basin Commission's recreation maps grew a lifetime love of maps and the geographical imagination. These river maps listed the rapids and their difficulty, the islands and towns, channels and their depths, bridges and boat ramps. But a river is always less static than a map, constantly moving, the bank and islands adding and subtracting, new rocks in rapids, making new waves.

I knew my little home stretch of river well, starting when I was young and learning to swim. There were big, submerged rocks that we kids would stumble into, stand on so water was knee high, dive from. We learned to know all the bumps in our section, from our floating dock to the next upstream neighbors, the Millers. Then the longer section of town, a few rocks to be avoided, lest a propeller blade shear off. My dad had a wall of these torn-up props, used in the service of better knowing and "mapping" the river.

We pick up scars along the way—in the service of learning, we hope.

On recent visits, I see new rocks in the old swimming hole, a few new buoys to mark the rogue rocks in the wider river, dislodged by ice or flood. It changes but doesn't change. We leave it but it doesn't leave us.

If I knew that home stretch, I used to think I would want to know the whole thing, every other little segment. But a river is a wide watershed of topography and vegetation and all the tributaries that feed the river, the little trickling streams that feed those. The source is never finite, nor is the end. I can't of course know it all, but here again a river is a metaphor. I can know some of it very well, and certainly learn as much as I can about these two hundred miles between me and home. "You can comprehend a piece of river," writes John Graves in *Goodbye to a River*, a book I read just as the pandemic lockdown ensued. It fit the tone of the moment: weary, troubled, isolated.

He was saying goodbye to the Brazos, soon (in the 1950s) to be dammed. I don't have an urgent reason for being here, such as seeing the river for the last time. It's more that I want to see it for the first time all over again. And it's not that I want to test myself in the wild (and scenic). I'm well aware of that narrative too. I'm here mostly out of curiosity, to check in with myself and this river that has run throughout my childhood and life.

Besides, I've paddled segments of it, but never the whole thing continuously. I dislike the term "bucket list"—things to do before one kicks the bucket. As if we need a reason to attempt otherwise "daring" things only if framed in the face of death. Would not fun and curiosity be enough? The pandemic reminded all of us of our need for connection with others and with the flow and movement of things outside.

I took one of my first canoe trips on a summer afternoon when I was twelve. Some neighbors gathered and borrowed some of Abbott's Marine canoes, the big heavy aluminum Grumman kind. They weren't the artful birchbarks of old and lacked refinement and were instead manufactured after the war as Grumman sought business beyond aerospace. But they brought boats to the masses that were nearly indestructible, if famous for getting hung up. Aluminum may be a good, cheap material to rivet into a canoe shape, but it lacks glide, often leaving silver marks on rocks. Punctures could be fixed with more rivets or solder.

We piled into boats, me proudly steering from the stern. My mother packed some cold chicken we ate on the silty bank. I tried to mimic my older neighbors Bob Miller and Jim Abbott, navigate through the riffles so as not to hang up, learning to read the water and downward-facing V. Grace, power, control. It's an afternoon I remember to this day: sparkling water, paddle T-grip in hand, sunbaked seats. In my teens, when my father's business went belly-up, we went canoeing rather than take some expensive vacation. In my early twenties, three friends and I drove all night to Narrowsburg, putting in at fog-lifting dawn, eating psychedelic mushrooms at dusk. Thirty, a trip with the woman I would marry, following some cedar waxwings around a bend. In my forties, some trips with my kids, pretending that I was injured and that my son and his friend would have to canoe me out, à la Burt Reynolds/Lewis in *Deliverance*. We spied a falcon under the Scudders Falls Bridge, saw an osprey dive, watched that incredible focused intensity, headlong for water then flip position to feet first, splash, clutch wriggling fish, regroup and fly off, high-pitched screeching over the catch. Ospreys, falcons, eagles—all part of the comeback of the river. All part of the reason I've returned, come back, in my fifties. Though I'm more a bird enthusiast than an expert. For that matter, I'm more a canoe and camping enthusiast than an expert.

Trips begot other trips, and taught me this much: do your best, bring what you need, prepare for the journey ahead, and hope not to be dashed on the rocks downstream. If you do flip, hang in there with the boat until you can find an eddy and place on shore to empty the water.

The river made a place in two of my three books—now it gets its own. When I finished the first, based on a dissertation twenty-five years ago, I made a file of things that might be my next project, calling it "River." In that project on literary cartography, I mused on the geographic border I saw out my bedroom window. On maps, a fixed line, but my border moved. And in a project about getting kids outside, experiencing wonder, I talked about finding swimming holes (beginning with my first), days on the river in boats, a fishing-birding-swimming picnic. My last dealt with climate change in the South, so the river was excluded, but with me in spirit, as I visited the "birthplace of rivers" in West Virginia. And sleeping beside one, I drank in the murmur of a river, faint gurgle, hiss and hum.

That book covered the climate circumstances in seven southern states and one mountainous one, involving a lot of travel through a wide expanse. The climate situation will worsen in the coming years, and we are already seeing effects on rivers like the Delaware, with increased rainfall and flooding (drought in the West). But rather than wrap my head around such an extensive region, or problem, I aim to zero in. One question I continue to ask, in the wake of that travel to climate-afflicted regions, is how do we care for a place in a time of upheaval and loss?

All three projects relate to the sense of place, the specific conditions of topography and climate and culture that make places unique, worthy of attention. And for the way they reach deep inside us. When I return to my hometown, the first thing I do, before the greetings or hugs, is walk to the bank and look at the river, where there is so much to learn: the water level based on the large rock we could not dislodge, the recent rains based on the color and speed of the current, and just the silty scent will release a surge of memory and association. I've brought all those I've loved there, and in some ways it was a first love, a place of birth. A place to begin again.

This story has yet another origin. Two years before the date of this trip I fell down. I began that August morning ready to get back to work and school. I had syllabi to prepare and an annual report to finish. Emails to catch up on at my writing desk. But my left hand was not cooperating, and I, nauseous, tried to make my way to the couch, when my left foot gave out. I tried to pull myself up, using the leg of a chair, but only the right arm would grab. I had no idea what was happening, but the medics my wife and daughter called confirmed that I had had, was having, a transient ischemic attack, a small stroke. I was flown to a Roanoke hospital where they had an emergency stroke center. The doctor inserted something like nitroglycerin into my femoral artery and watched my blood vessels on a monitor, like a river and its tributaries. The dyed material traveled up to the clot, halted, then up around the brain through something called the circle of Willis, and attacked from the top. The dam in the vessels dislodged. When it did, I squeezed the doctor's hand and opened my eyes.

Sometime that summer, or just days before, I had "dissected" my right internal carotid artery, meaning I had developed a small tear. This usually happens to those who experience whiplash, but I could remember no such event. The tear was like a kink in a hose, and the clot was helping with the repair, but when a piece of that shot up, I went down. During a right-sided stroke you are barely aware of what is happening, and notoriously, among family and friends, I was dubious of the severity. About the helicopter, I made the "it will cost money" sign with my thumb and forefinger. I've always been calm in stressful situations and remained so horizontally on a stretcher to the hospital and into the helicopter. When it lifted up and over the Blue Ridge Mountains, I strained my injured neck to look at the folds and ridges below. Tucked into the shadows—flowing water, the sources of rivers. You can't have them without mountains. I'm not sure if I was simply sneaking a peek, but perhaps, like nature writers John Muir and Ralph Waldo Emerson—who both nearly lost their sight—vowed I would see and do all that I could, savoring the view, the very moment.

I seemed to have made a full recovery, but days after, I discovered I had blurred vision in one eye—possible optic nerve damage. Moments later, some good friends showed up in my hospital room, and though the eye wasn't working as it should, the tear ducts still did. The realization had hit me that it all could have been much, much worse.

I won't be walking to the Gulf of Mexico, like Muir, but I will be taking this trip. I set out by myself two years from the anniversary of the fall, and once again a year later with the Lenape Nation of Pennsylvania, who make the trip every four years as the Rising Nation River Journey. I learned about their trip late in the summer, when trying to find more stories about people and the river. Having seen it all by myself, I wanted to see it as others did, and who better to learn from about the history and health of the river than the first people who lived on and tended it?

Floating a river, you realize the ways its story meanders into one's own. Rapids, eddies, and islands are the risks, pauses, and periods of isolation one experiences in a life. Rifts in the river relate to other personal or cultural fissures. Rivers change and heal themselves, as they are themselves healing.

You can't go home again, famously, nor can you step in the same river twice, but you can return to the scene of a crime, of love, of happiness. Places and rivers remain and, even if changed, or altered, are what is immortal. Now to float some of that fluttering wing.

Sunrise on the East Branch at railroad bridge in Hancock, New York.

CONFLUENCE

Day 1—Hancock to Equinunk
330–322

What are the chances? What are the chances the woman in the Circle E Diner in Hancock also had a stroke? I finished my lunchtime BLT, the last food someone might prepare for me in a while, and was trying to find the put-in on my phone. So I asked the friendly waitress, Danielle. She gave directions the way people used to, down this road and right on the gravel road and past the wastewater facility, just south of town.

I asked for the name of the ramp, and she pulled over her coworker, but she didn't know the name either. When you live there, it's just the ramp you use, and Danielle used it often, thirty-two times last year.

"Why so often?"

"Because I love that river, and kayaking is therapy."

Danielle, a grandmother, though younger than me by the looks of it, described a connective tissue disease that resulted in several surgeries, including to the brain, and not one but two strokes.

"I've had one too," I told her, and then where I was headed. Two hundred miles downriver.

She relayed her long medical history good-naturedly, even pleasantly, smiling, as if glad to tell her story. Glad that someone was interested in more than just her ability to refill iced teas, sling plates.

"Be careful," my mother warned. "You could be in a book."

"You're a writer?"

"I write, and yeah, might write about this trip." I am reluctant to say I'm a writer in diners.

She told me she wanted to write two books. One about her struggles with her disease, and another about etiquette.

"Etiquette?" I started thinking back on how I acted during my meal.

"Yeah, how people behave, especially in here. They can be so rude."

"So a book on kindness?"

"Yes."

In an act of kindness, she had given my dog Sully, tied to the railing outside, a little cup of whipped cream. Then she pointed us toward the river and ramp. The fair was in town, and Danielle, who hears things at the diner, told us that Calvin had found a purple pearl in one of the clams at Fireman's Field Days.

My seventy-seven-year-old mother, Elene, was my "shuttle bunny," a term obviously out of favor, but once defined by *Canoe and Kayak* magazine as "a non-paddling person who agrees to run shuttle. Shuttle bunnies who wait at the takeout with cold beer (without drinking it) are urban myths." She also ordered the BLT, ate it slowly with slender, age-spotted hands, slumping in the Naugahyde booth across from me, peering through glasses under gray bangs.

We drove three hours from Titusville up Route 31, an old road we used to take every winter to get to the Poconos to ski. We passed many changes, a lot of new Central Jersey development, but also some familiar landmarks, like the Luigi's where we once stopped after a day of skiing, someone falling asleep on the bench, their meatballs unfinished. And Hot Dog Johnny's, still there, birch beer and buttermilk in frosted mugs, hard to pass up (not the buttermilk). We played Scrabble late into the night with my daughter who happened to be around, visiting friends in Philadelphia, looking for work, ready to begin life after college.

After college I once thought I would return to that river town, Titusville, and people once lived in the areas they were raised, but I was pulled away by middle-class and very American (and problematic) assumptions about moving on. We continued up through the Delaware Water Gap and into the Poconos, making our way to the river, losing confidence in our GPS, my mother a map reader without a map. I notice her dry humor, share her love of maps. The scenery is Pennsylvania, but it might as well be Vermont, green and mountainous, and the thought always occurs in places such as this: who lives here, and what do they do for work? They do something, and likely found their way here by family and association, a rootedness. I am of an academic tribe, one of those who choose where to live (or are chosen), rather than settling among family, connection. I looked out on some leaning barns, faded farmhouses, with a little longing.

≈ ≈ ≈

One hundred and thirty years ago, in 1892, J. Wallace Hoff and four other canoeists hatched the idea to paddle the whole river from its headwaters to where they sat, on a porch near what was then Park Island (now Rotary), overlooking the river, the "ceaseless surging of Trenton Falls" heard in the distance. Hoff and men tossed "uneasily" on cots that night, "troubled by visions of swift currents and foam-lashed falls, with which they were battling in a journey down the Delaware from its headwaters to its tide."

I tossed some as well, partly in anticipation but also in doing the mental check of gear. Tents and stakes. Paddles and life jackets. I couldn't remember if I'd packed the orange one for Sully. The whole question of whether to bring her was also a concern. She had been with me on several pilot runs, but how would she do for a whole day or days? A Catahoula mix, her coat is mostly black with a patchwork of white and tan, spotted and piebald around her face and belly. She liked to check out the waterfowl on the left and then those on the right, meaning I had to counterbalance. Would she tip the boat in a rapid? She might also provide some companionship and might even help when it came time to talk with people. Ease the conversation. Nothing says responsible and trustworthy like a dog owner, right? Graves brought his along in *Goodbye to a River*, called Passenger. John Steinbeck had his Charley. Sully would come, and I hoped the life jacket was buried in the trunk somewhere.

Hoff and crew had camp blankets, tents, cots, cooking utensils, skeleton and oil stoves, lanterns, hatchets, and toilet bags. They also had a plate camera, fishing "implements," and a pistol. They shipped this to

Hancock by train, and some of it arrived in less-than-ideal condition, the camera warped slightly, some tackle missing, and the pistol, harmed by some moisture, rendering a "self-cocking, rapid-firing, self-ejector as harmless as some cannon of General Washington's."

I brought a fishing rod. After all, that section near Hancock and the branches above it are hallowed waters for anglers, and widely considered to be the birthplace of fly-fishing in the United States. But I brought no pistol. Every Memorial and Labor Day weekend for about a five-year stretch I would pile some gear, including fishing gear, in a canoe, and paddle a section of the New River in Virginia, where I now live. I loved the feeling of taking all I'd need for a weekend and packing it in the boat. With me would be my son Sam, fishing off the bow, and a friend Bob and his son in their canoe. Bob is former military, was also a pilot, and some of his training comes to bear on his choice of both site and gear selection.

He wanted to make sure we camped where no one would bother us. We even one time did an aerial reconnaissance of some islands on the river to look at their suitability. And he brought a pistol, showing me the combo on the waterproof box, "in case someone does come into camp."

I wasn't so much worried about someone coming into camp as I was misfiring a dangerous weapon or escalating a situation that didn't need to escalate. Howdy, friend? How about a beverage? My style tends more toward the minimalist, something he and I laugh over. "Minimalist just means you're willing to put up with a certain degree of discomfort." I see it as a way to pare down to the essential, a Zen-like focus more on the experience, the view, nature. Bob is laughing as I type this.

Hoff's canoe was an open Watertown hunting canoe, fourteen feet in length, ten inches in depth, "smooth skin, covered with oiled canvas." A Watertown canoe was likely made in Watertown, New York (St. Lawrence County), at one time birchbark. He wrote that it was the "first open canoe paddled on the Delaware at Trenton," weighing fifty-five pounds.

I found one of these online, AntiqueBoatAmerica.com, fourteen feet and fifty-five pounds, for $6,000. Tempting, but opted instead for my sixteen-foot Wenonah Adirondack, Royalex rather than bark/canvas. Royalex is a composite vinyl and foam, firm yet forgiving and even slippery when you scrape, and not too heavy. My boat weighed about as much as Hoff's, with more volume. It hails from Winona, Minnesota, on a bluff above the Mississippi. Twenty-five years old, it has seen quite a bit of use, frequently carrying two adults, two children, and often a dog. Like the forehead of Herman Melville's whale, the hull bears the scars and hieroglyphics of time, each telling a story.

Hoff called his boat the *Nahiwi,* a Lenape word for "downstream." I was still thinking of a name when I kept seeing mergansers, cinnamon-brown heads. The shaggy crown resembled the maroon of my boat. Merganser somehow reminded me of Murgatroyd, and how the pink cougar Snagglepuss used to say, "heavens to Murgatroyd." I started calling my boat Margaret. Or simply Marge, which rhymed with barge.

We drove to Hancock, but Hoff and company took the train to Jersey City, running into the arched terminal station of the Pennsylvania Railroad, the interior flooded with light. Then, it was the largest railroad station in the world. They debarked and took a ferry into New York, walking among fish stalls, poultry booths, cheap restaurants, and "groggeries." From these came a few "down-at-the-heel and blear-eyed roustabouts, wiping away the burning spray after a nip of questionable character." Then back across the river and another train to Port Jervis and then Hancock.

They found the town a "dusty place among the hills," with three large hotels. One of them, the Hancock Hotel, is still in operation, though at a different site. At the foot of Point Mountain, below a small rift, they packed their "impedimenta." I did too, after finding the place with Danielle's directions, and in a hurry to get on the water and wanting my shuttle runner, looking a little more diminutive and brittle each year, on the road home before dark. I hugged her and the hump below her neck. Luckily, the dog PFD had been packed.

Point Mountain rose tall in the distance, the East and West Branches merging around it. I pushed off at this confluence—one of reflection and expectation too. Any departure blends a little of what came before with some promise of the day to come.

Hoff and crew dipped cups over the edge of their boats and drank "cups of clean—yes clean—wholesome water, from mountain streams fed by other streams," drinking too the air, "pure fresh mountain air, swept from hills of spruce and pine." I too was grateful for the air, and clear water, though I did not drink from the river directly, since I was sharing it with the wildlife I saw sipping from the banks and wanted to avoid "beaver fever" (giardiasis). I also was not leaving an industrial city behind, nor an environment before clean water or air laws.

≈ ≈ ≈

It was in Jersey City, where Hoff and company took a ferry to New York, that we first figured out how to treat public water. John L. Leal was born in Andes, New York, graduated from Princeton, and earned a medical degree from Columbia. He opened a practice in Paterson, New Jersey, later becoming the city's physician. His father, John R. Leal, also a doctor, joined the 144th New York Volunteer Infantry Regiment during the Civil War and contracted a chronic case of amoebic dysentery—most likely from contaminated drinking water—at Folly Island, South Carolina, from which he suffered for nearly twenty years before succumbing to the disease. Around the time Hoff and crew crossed the Hudson into Manhattan, Leal was appointed as Paterson's health officer. In that role, he identified communicable diseases and their causes. He also oversaw the public water supply and was responsible for constructing the growing network of sewers to remove domestic and industrial wastes. He later became the sanitary adviser to the East Jersey Water Company.

As a physician trained in microbiology, Leal knew that chlorine killed bacteria. As health officer for Paterson, Leal used solutions of chloride to disinfect homes where scarlet fever, diphtheria, and other communicable diseases were found. He was also aware of previous efforts to use chlorine in drinking water supplies, to kill dangerous microbes. As adviser to the water company, Leal quietly added chlorine to the public reservoirs in Jersey City. The city sued, saying Leal had failed to provide the "pure and wholesome" water his contract stipulated. Leal ultimately won the case, and typhoid deaths dropped precipitously. Other cities, including Chicago and Detroit, followed suit, and by 1914, 50 percent of public water systems were supplying disinfected water. Today, half of New York City's drinking water drains from reservoirs in the Delaware River watershed and runs through the eighty-five-mile-long Delaware Aqueduct, the longest tunnel in the world. According to the New York City Department of Environmental Protection's water quality report, it all ends in Yonkers, where it is not filtered, but is treated with chlorine.

Hoff and company made the mountains "ring with our overflowing spirits." I was in good spirits too, with forested ridges heaving skyward on both sides of the river. These hills, part of the Appalachian Plateau, were once heavily logged, but were now clothed in secondary hardwoods, green hillsides rising toward a swatch of blue. Yellow goldenrod, blindingly bright, and purple Joe Pye weed, stately in August bloom, buzzed and swayed on the banks. The river is narrower and shallower than at home, maybe two country roads side by side. It is swifter too, but clear, and I was soon mesmerized by the gravelly bottom, by all shapes and sizes, the smooths and serrateds, ovals and oblongs—grays, browns, tans, black and white, seeming to wear expressions. Fish like such cobble, where they lay eggs, and more than one scooted for safety. The boat threw a shadow, and my paddle a wake in the water.

Another physician who spent time in Paterson, also a poet, William Carlos Williams would write in "Good Night" about turning on the kitchen spigot, watching the water "plash" into the clean white sink. While waiting for "the water to freshen" in his glass, he is transported by memory "playing the clown," to girls in "crimson satin," an opera, high school French, until the water in the glass brings him back. He takes a drink, yawns, and is ready for bed, when the poet is presumably back in a dream. While paddling, and staring at the water, I too got lost in a reverie, and until something brought me back to myself, to the present. Water transports us as much as we it, transpires through us, "freshens" before our daydreaming eyes.

I had never been here but the river felt familiar in a strange, nourishing way. Thoughts receded into the background as the landscape—shoreline, skyline—begged attention. I stroked some on the left, then on the right. I anticipated I would camp sometimes on my left (New York), and maybe on my right (Pennsylvania), or on an island right down the middle. I pulled on the straight wooden shaft of the paddle, smooth with varnish, epoxy tip. Water dripped from the flat blade. A slight breeze came up, creating ripples in the water and filtering the light, and it occurred to me that I had no other purpose than to let the wind blow through the day, which felt like as good a purpose as any.

A few fishermen were out, one or two that I snuck up on. A canoe is quiet, and the afternoon river was still. Sometimes a brief slap on the hull. If sound, the murmurous sound of water, the paddle stirring the water. Or my fingers swirling it, pleasing chill.

The other boats had decent luck, and a guide netted a bass just as I drifted past. Other fish catchers were hidden in the trees. Eagles may be majestic in flight, but their call is somewhat weak. I heard some high whistles, piping notes, but the birds stayed hidden for now.

Ten or more years before Hoff, the naturalist and writer John Burroughs made a trip from his home down the East Branch, which he called Pepacton, a Lenape name meaning "marriage of the waters." He describes it as "draining a high pastoral country lifted into long, round-backed hills and rugged, wooded ranges by the subsiding impulse" of the Catskill Mountains, famous for its dairy farms. In "A Summer Voyage," published in 1881, he crafts his own wooden boat, fishes for trout in the spring-fed tributaries, shelters from the rain under wooden bridges or slate barn roofs, and asks farm wives for milk in his pail, not skimmed please. He meets people along the way, as I do, and birds aplenty: kingbirds giving chase to eagles, whip-poor-wills as he lay down at night, song sparrows and cuckoos as well. In the morning, robins, orioles, catbirds, wrens, a wood thrush, and "all the rest of the tuneful choir." At dawn the birds build and tend nests, "the back of their day's work is broken before you have begun yours." He gives chase to a heron and a rooster joins him in the shed, safe from the storm before he chases it off. He eats wild strawberries and fresh trout, washed down with fresh farmer's milk. A summer idyll for an idler.

Burroughs was immensely popular in his day and maintained friendships with Walt Whitman, John Muir, and Theodore Roosevelt. He was also well-liked by industrialists, including Henry Ford, who gave Burroughs a Model T in hopes he would endorse the vehicle as a pleasing way to see nature, rather than as a "steel monster." Naturalist Burroughs and industrialists Ford, Thomas Edison, and Harvey Firestone would all car-camp together in style, calling themselves the Vagabonds. They helped give birth to the great American road trip, touring burgeoning roadways through the Adirondacks, Smokies, Everglades, and the California coast. The group had to cancel the tour due to the attention they attracted and, ultimately, Burroughs's ailing health. Instead, the traveling companions visited him at his cabin in the Catskills. Riverby, by the Hudson, was Burroughs's homestead, but he built a cabin a couple of miles west modeled after Thoreau, calling it Slabsides, after the bark-covered sheathings of the logs it was made from. "Life has a different flavor here," he wrote, in *Far and Near*. "It is reduced to simpler terms; its complex equations all disappear."

Burroughs's career took the opposite arc of Thoreau's, as he was popular when writing but is little read today. He may not plumb the depths as much as the Concord philosopher and is perhaps not as radical in his eco-centered views. Though he lacks some of Thoreau's method for extracting meaning from nature, there is much to admire in the delight and joy he finds in it, and he may have been the superior naturalist. Burroughs thought Thoreau a dreamer, an idealist, and a "fervid ethical teacher." If Thoreau saw something unusual in nature, Burroughs said, "he must need to draw some moral from it and indulge his passion for striking expression and fantastic comparison, usually at the expense of the truth." In "A Critical Glance into Thoreau," the Catskill naturalist wrote that the Concord one was "too intent upon the bird behind the bird always to take careful note of the bird itself."

At the confluence in Hancock, Burroughs finds nearly a dozen ospreys, and in the long deep eddy comes upon a "brood of wild ducks," though his were the hooded merganser, with a fancy hoody, a bouffant do, and the ones I encounter, in the same area, are the common variety, though they seem anything but "common"—a word that could connote vulgar, ordinary, or low. He watches them wheel away on their feet, no need for wings, walking on water. "I dropped my paddle and cheered."

≈ ≈ ≈

I heard an occasional rumble of a car on the road, but mostly the splash of these mergansers as I also cheered their takeoff: *fwap, fwap, fwap* of feet on water spinning like a steamboat wheel, breast just lifting off, and then a whir of wings. Their call bounces across the water like a cross between a frog and a duck. Audubon called them the "buff-breasted merganser" in his *The Birds of America* and also "goosander," which the British still do. Merganser comes from the Latin words *mergus* (diver) and *anser* (goose)—a plunging goose.

I saw more fish here than I did at any point in the river. They appeared as oval shadows turning and fleeing. I saw more fishermen too. The question I wanted to pose to people I met is something like, "what brings you to the river?" Or, "what does the river mean to you?" Or simply, "why the river?"

I thought I might fish and look for a camp at Equinunk Creek. Though the river is designated wild and scenic on this stretch, the land is mostly private. There was supposed to be a camp just up the creek, and if signs had pointed me in that direction, I might have headed there. I had recalled reading that Equinunk was Lenape for "place of lots of fish" or something similar, but I could not verify that. In fact, it is Lenape for "place where cloth is distributed." Which explains why I saw no fish. Or camp.

I would learn later, on the return trip, that Equinunk meant, more specifically, the place where cloth is laid, as in out to dry, like on a riverbank. Carol Ann Macmaster of the Historical Society of Equinunk told me this at the Calder House Museum. Shelley DePaul, of the Lenape Nation of Pennsylvania, confirmed it. Shelley is the assistant chief and education and language director of the nation. Every four years since 2002, they have made a Rising Nation River Journey, Hancock to Cape May, to bring awareness to the fact that there are still Lenape in the Lenapehoking, the place of the Lenape (their territory included parts of the Delaware, Lehigh, Hudson, and Susquehanna river valleys), and their sacred river, the Lenape Sipu, or Delaware. "Delaware" is of course not of Indigenous origin. Shelley told me that "Lenape" translates to "original people," and they have been around for some ten thousand years.

A year after my first trip, I set out with them on a summer morning from Hancock and around noon we parked our boats on the Equinunk bank, walked up the creek, past an old hotel with bar, as people with the museum greeted us from the porch. Inside, they fed us lunch. After we ate, I walked around the museum, filled with pioneer artifacts, such as quilts and looms, and old furniture and kitchen utensils. In the basement, however, there is a dugout canoe. And a sign: "Records indicate that by 1769 there were only two families of the Delaware tribes in the area." "Throughout these centuries," the plaque continued, "some remained in Pennsylvania, marrying and assimilating. These ancestors hid their Native American heritage to protect their children from persecution. Only in the last few decades has it been possible for the descendants of those ancestors to begin to practice their religion and culture again. Although many say there are no Indians in the East, in truth there are thousands of them." Some of them were upstairs eating barbeque.

After lunch, the historical society, and anyone else, was welcome to sign a treaty of renewed friendship. It's not a legally binding treaty, not that treaties with Indigenous people ever were, but something to acknowledge the Lenape as the original caretakers of these lands and river and to agree to support the Lenape culture. The treaty reads: "In the spirit of Chief Tamanend and in the spirit of William Penn, we, the undersigned, do openly recognize the Lenape Indian Tribe as the original inhabitants of Pennsylvania. We acknowledge the Lenape people as the indigenous stewards of their homelands and also as the spiritual keepers of the Lenape Sipu, or Delaware River."

In his appendix, Hoff included "A Little Bit of History," with remarks on the discovery by Hudson and purchase of the South River by the Swedes from the "original owners" of the land—the Lenape. He continues to write that it was on account of the "equitable and just purchase from the rightful owner" that Pennsylvania, through William Penn, "enjoyed the immunity from that Indian distrust which was so marked in those other sections seized and usurped by the early settlers." In letters to England, Penn, who the Lenape called Brother Onas or just Onas (writing quill or one who writes), said the Lenape were a peaceable nation. The Treaty of Shackamaxon, also called the Great Treaty or Penn's Treaty, was a legendary treaty between William Penn and Chief Tamanend of the Lenape signed in present-day Philadelphia in 1682. Penn and Tamanend agreed that their people would live in a state of perpetual peace. They mostly would for some fifty years.

Hoff generally seems sympathetic to the Lenape, their plight, and notes that the "last remnant migrated to Ohio in the year 1800." He describes their three major clans, the Munsee (Minsi) tribe, with the wolf as totem, that inhabited the area above Easton, with council fires at the Water Gap and the Minisink plains (Port Jervis area). Then the Unami, or Turtle tribe, from the Lehigh to the Trenton Falls. Chief Chuck Gentlemoon De-Mund, who led the morning ceremony, was an Unami. And finally, the Unilachtego, Turkey tribe, who occupied lands near the ocean, Philadelphia to Wilmington. Adam Waterbear DePaul, Shelley's son and coordinator of the Lenape trip, told me that because they bore the first and most contact from early settlers, their population was hit the hardest.

On the first trip in 2002, the group had about seventeen historical and preservation societies sign. Twenty years later, some fifty groups had pledged support, so the nation really was rising.

Jim Beer, who had the idea for the original trip, told me the treaty was first introduced as a kind of joke. "Should we have people sign something?" But then they thought, why not? And rather than use the river to divide, as it does states in the region, let's use it to bring people together. Jim brought his sons, Tamanend, named after the chief, and Ahlankw (ah-LON-qua), a Lenape word for star. Ahlankw was just two months old on the first trip, but he met paddlers somewhere near the Water Gap and they baptized him. Miqwan (Lenape for feather), Jim's young daughter, rode in the kayak with him.

Shelley said that it was on one of the Lenape river trips that the idea came to her to work to resurrect the language. Lenape is of the Algonquin family, was an oral language and not written down, except sometimes through missionaries trying to translate the Bible and convert. At the time, Shelley was earning a master's in Irish history, studying some Gaelic, "because I think you need to know the language of the culture you are studying." She realized she didn't know the language of her own culture, such as translations for place names she was traveling through. She has made it her life's work to revive the language and teaches classes online and at Swarthmore College.

We had about thirty boats on the trip (three weeks later, it was fifty). Some were members of the nation and some just wanted to come along for the journey. Some were in Shelley's classes, although she was not on the water this year and was instead helping with the ground crew. Adam Waterbear DePaul, burly in his sleek sea kayak, piercings under his life jacket and lower lip, is earning a doctorate in English from Temple University. Between puffs on a cigarette dangling from his mouth, he told me that there was no "blood" requirement to join the nation, but they do require some proof of genealogy.

≈ ≈ ≈

On my solo trip, I kept paddling, hoping for a campsite. The river turned some, and I hugged the Pennsylvania shore, staring up into the hemlock forest. Around a bend, I saw two women in the water, and then two on a grassy knoll above them. One sat in a tube, holding a rope tied to a tree, and another, with a big floppy sun hat, stood upon seeing me.

Her eyes grew wide. "You're my husband. Look at you," she said, with a British accent, all surprise, and little laughter from her and the others.

I slowed, not sure what to say.

"Come over here. Who are you?" she continued. I spun the canoe so it was just downstream from them, the bow now held by the bank.

"I'm on a river trip. Heading downriver. What brings you guys to the river?"

The British woman, Trish, continued: "We're on a river trip too." More laughter. "Smokin' doobies and eating shrooms."

Sherri sat in the tube while her sister, Theresa, lounged up on blankets with Daryl, the owner of the property. None of us were sure what to say next, but I asked if I could let Sully out, and if their dog Conroy, a stout pit mix, would play. Soon they were chasing each other through the woods, over the blankets and towels. No one minded much.

Sherri asked me my dog's name. She wore a camo ball cap and sleeveless shirt, dangled her legs and sandals over the tube. "Sully" sounded Irish to Daryl, who is from Ireland. She covered a bathing suit with a tan linen button-down and wore a necklace of turquoise beads. I told them I got Sully on the day Toni Morrison died, which made me think of Sula, Morrison's unconventional heroine, and Sula became Sully.

"So you're a writer?" Sherri asked.

"And English teacher."

"What do you write?"

I told them. Last book was about climate change in the South. Someone said Sherri wrote too.

"What do you write?"

She didn't want to say. It was in progress and she felt that talking about it too much would somehow put pressure on it, jinx it in some way. I could relate but offered that I was hoping to write about this trip.

"I feel more comfortable writing down what I want to say rather than speaking it."

I could relate to that too.

"And I need time. I can't seem to write without an unfettered block of time."

Hear, hear! While the dogs continued to run, I offered one of the beers from my cooler. Sherri took one. They were impressed with my setup. My green canoe seat with back, the black box that contained most of my cooking supplies and food, the gray waterproof duffel that held my tent and sleeping bag. All of it strapped to the thwarts. I joined them on the grass overlooking the river.

"How far are you going?"

Daryl had no idea where Trenton was.

Sherri: "Are you just doing it or are you going through something?"

Good question, but I deflected. "Aren't we all going through something?"

They wanted to know more. Did I have kids? I did—two, both just out of college.

Daryl has two too, and this led to how different it feels when older. "They're the center of your lives for a while, but then they separate from you. And you've got to figure it out. It's no longer just taking them from here to there."

I learned that the four had not gathered in a long time. This was a reunion of sorts. And that Daryl had started coming here with her husband, Paul, to get away from the city some twenty-five years ago. I would later learn that Daryl was a fashion designer known for something called the hip-hugger bootleg jean. Place where cloth is made? Pretty soon their escapes from the city grew longer and longer yet, until they stayed. When they first arrived, they knew it was something special. "I mean look at it."

It both was and was not. I mean I've seen some spectacular rivers and I'd traveled down the Middle Fork of the Salmon earlier that summer and the Green River in Utah a few summers before. There was scenery on a grander scale, but it was a beauty that blares at you. This whispered. Less Notre Dame than a small stone chapel in the hills. It is a lovely and peaceful stretch of river, with a grassy, ferny bank overlooking it, a hardwood and hemlock forest breathing nearby, its shadows reflecting in the surface at water's edge. And what made it even better? This river, this one right here, was a strand that ran right by my boyhood home. An eagle called in the distance.

Our conversation kept getting more personal. Was I single? What was it like? How do you meet people? Daryl liked the idea of online dating: "At least you don't have to meet when drunk."

But no one was a fan of online teaching. Theresa didn't like it at all for her Montessori classes. She asked if I wanted some black bean salad. I hesitated. Was I overstaying a welcome? But I said sure.

"What a lucky stroke," said Daryl, who had no idea.

More questions. How'd I get to Hancock? My mother. Did I love her? Sure did. We agreed that we preferred real human talk to the online thing, "like this, like me with you," said Daryl. She reminded me of an actress I couldn't place. Part Gillian Anderson, part Kate Winslet. She wanted to write a book too (the third author of the day), maybe one about climate change from the perspective of the animals it was affecting. "But then it would be a talking animal book." More laughter. "Yes, then it would be a talking animal book," said Trish.

Trish wanted to know my sign, which I gave (Capricorn). "Ah, makes sense," she said, in that knowing way people who read astrology find relevance in these things.

I said I was dubious. And that made horoscopic sense too. I am a curiosity to them, they to me. Theresa came down from the house above and served the black bean salad on a porcelain platter. Caprese salad too with sprigs of basil. Better than what I packed. The last fresh for 192 miles? More talk, on the menopause of whales. I had no idea, but it made sense to me in a way horoscopes did not.

We also talked of eagle rescue, which Sherri and Theresa engaged in. Sherri had an eagle on her T-shirt and a tattoo of one, a geometric abstract, near her shoulder. They can ingest lead from gut piles and get sick or die.

How do I help students cope with climate grief? The latest IPCC (Intergovernmental Panel on Climate Change) report had just come out, the sixth. I gave them my best answer. That I try to make sure students understand the facts, but that there are solutions. As much as a scientific or engineering problem, it's the human engineering that's hard to bring around. That will take community and creativity. Real talk. "But I don't want to be too negative to shut them down. They have to fall in love too, with a place. Or a river (wink)."

Trish sensed our conversation getting too heavy. She told about being happily inappropriate in serious situations. She was in Jamaica once and crashed a party to "get some boogie." We all thought she said "booty," but Trish, "I'm a lady (wink)." She dances and dances and says to the host, "you sure do throw a good party," and he, "this is my wife's funeral."

I shared more beer, and they passed around the smoke. I was starting to worry about where I'd make camp. Daryl said there was a Russian guy at the next bridge who "threw parties," and he would probably let me crash. I could ask him. But that didn't seem real definite.

Daryl and I continued on the thread of horoscopes, my dubiousness, and whether the "universe" cohered to some plan, sent us messages. "No one has come through here in twenty-five years, and then you." I doubted that—it was just that no one had come through when they were on the bank, probably around dusk, like now. Trish, recently divorced, had mentioned that she went out in the water to "open herself to the universe," and there I was.

Daryl believed there was an "energy," an order, which I could grant. I had been flowing on one all day, or they had. But could we know it? "We can intuit," she said. "It's not all rational out there."

It was/is an old conversation, and I rather enjoyed having it with these complete strangers. Do things happen for a reason, or do they just happen? I thought of it with the stroke. In *Everything Happens for a Reason: And Other Lies I've Loved*, Kate Bowler writes of how absurd this can sound to the cancer patient. Because of sin, or unfaithfulness. Because God is fair, or he/she is unfair. Because of an aversion to Brussels sprouts.

When I was in graduate school, the then Cleveland Indians (now Guardians) played the Yankees in the American League playoffs. A rookie pitcher, Jaret Wright, made his playoff debut. He won game two and started game five, both against Andy Petite. With her father, my wife, Catherine, had watched years of "tribe" futility against the Yanks. She made a "pact with the universe" that our unborn son, due in two months, would be named Jaret if they won. After a premature and harrowing delivery, she told me of this pact. I was forty-eight hours into a seventy-two-hour comprehensive exam, holding forth on Melville and whales and interpretation. In our sleep-addled state, I told her, there in the spare hospital room, that the pact was "Ahabism," that the whale didn't "smite" Ahab specifically, that it just did what whales do. We laughed about it later, my professoring in the sterile room. But Jaret became Sam. And the Indians lost to the Marlins in the World Series anyway—the fish win again.

Little things, or accidents, can seem to have the weight and meaning of portents, or a confluence of forces. It's as though some force speaks to us, singles us out, and we haven't paid attention, but the signs were all there. Had we listened, and heeded the warnings, a different outcome. Surely a meaning "lurks" in all events, Ishmael muses, or the "round world itself but an empty cipher." More likely there is not a single meaning, but many, and they spool out like fuzzy ducklings trailing their mother.

Such were my thoughts on that afternoon on the river. The trees above reflected in the water, creating a symmetry, or the specter of one. Daryl's husband Paul had come down, finished with his workday, curry on the stove. After his swim, and while I was drying off from mine, Daryl told me that I could pitch my tent on the deck just above us. Paul said so, and "he's the man." More laughter.

I considered this. Thought about joining them for curry dinner, if invited. But I also had some inclination that this would take me too far from the river, some "purity" of the trip. Daryl took a few more stems and caps from an Altoids tin. Theresa and Sherri reminisced about a peyote ceremony their mother had joined.

≈ ≈ ≈

On the morning of the return trip with the Rising Nation River Journey, as we pulled our boats down to the waterline, Chuck Gentlemoon De-Mund, chief of ceremonies, looked up into the sky. He saw "the winged ones" and began a songful prayer in Lenape, shaking a rattle made from a turtle shell. We paused, turned to face him. Chuck embodies some of the duality of the modern Indian. In addition to a beaded headband to hold back long hair, he wore a ceremonial shirt on top, but below, silk boxing shorts and flip-flops. "What?" Chuck said, when finished his prayer, realizing he had our attention. "What are you all looking at?" he asked with a smirk.

Chuck can be both serious and ceremonial but also playful. On his car he had stickers for the Lenape Nation of Pennsylvania, of which he was a chief, but also the Philadelphia Flyers. "I just don't know what they're doing with that team," he told me, when I asked about the hockey season.

Before we began, Chuck told a story about how, when he was younger, he was nearly drowned in a tube. He now realized that it was not really his fault for not knowing the proper safety precautions, nor the river's fault either. Still, he had to respect it, feel humility. "My people believe we are no greater than the smallest ant."

Chief Chuck hit his drum and he said that it was like the heartbeat of the earth, and that the sound of it could take you back to the moment should you become lost. Then he led us in an acknowledgment of the creator, to look over us, and of the four directions, all of us turning to each as he spoke, first in Lenape language, then translated: east, of new beginnings, of spring; then south, summer, warmth, abundance; and west, of sundown, of that inevitable time; and north, of the white of elders, of wisdom, courage. After he finished, we joined him in *wanishi*, thank

you, twelve times, four groups of three. John Strongwind Martin, director of sacred sites, invited us to smudge. He had sage and cedar smoking
in a large abalone shell, and he fanned the aromatic smoke on us, head
to toe, with a hawk feather. They burned cedar because it was sacred to
the homeland; sage because the Lenape people couldn't find cedar when
they were removed west. Homeland and diaspora, burning in an irides-
cent shell there in his hand. The smudge would banish the bad thoughts,
bring on a good journey. When done in a community, it is quite calming.

When the group on the bank reminisced about their ceremony, I started
thinking about a place to camp. I opted for the other shore, a fishing camp
Daryl said was occupied only on weekends. Why exactly I left is hard to
say. Didn't want to impose more? Outstay my welcome? I might have
missed more time with my new best friends, Trish and I betrothed. Like
poet Robert Frost, I shall look back on this one day with a sigh, I chose
the side of the river less camped by. Made a pattern where there was none.
It wasn't a great choice, after all, because there were more mosquitos over
there.

When I did shove off, they wished me well on my journey. And I wished
them well on theirs.

Lower-level pontoon bridge, built in 1922

The Lordville-Equinunk bridge, built in 1992.

EDDIES

Day 2—Lordville to Narrowsburg
321–290

I slept well but it was also hard to forget that I was camped at someone's camp. When I heard noises, I feared I was about to be discovered, kicked out. I heard something that sounded like running, possibly a deer. And the mergansers or other waterfowl seemed to keep landing and taking off, splashdown, *karoonk*. These disturbed Sully greatly, who considered it her job to stay on alert inside the tent. And her bark, restlessness, made it harder to sleep. Late at night, when finally back in deep sleep, I startled to the sound of something picking through my food bag, so I jolted upright, grabbed my headlight to shine it on the culprit. Surely a racoon or worse, bear. It was Sully, licking the foil of her food package. I have friends who go all-in for gourmet gluten-free organic dog food, but among Sully's favorite foods is trash. A born scavenger, she will do about anything to get to food scraps. She had slipped out through a small opening in the tent's zipper.

I wanted a good night's sleep because I had much river to cover that day. Thirty miles, in fact. I had calculated that I would need to do about twenty-five miles a day, and I only traveled eight the first.

In the morning, I broke camp and paddled a short distance to the Lordville bridge. The original suspension bridge was built in 1869 by the Lord family, lost in a 1903 flood, rebuilt but demolished in 1986. The new bridge I stood on that morning was completed in 1992. My guide for the trip was a used 1985 version of *Canoeing the Delaware River: A Guide to the River and Shore* by Gary Letcher. Letcher had newer versions available, but this one was small and cheap, and I somehow liked that it was from the year I graduated high school. For the trip I had also purchased some of the Delaware River Basin Commission maps, made in 1966, the year I was born. Newer ones were available, but I liked that I might have been looking on the river as it (and I) once was. Besides, any good journey requires a degree of uncertainty.

Letcher wrote that the bridge was suspension and wood plank, but the one I stood on that morning with Sully was beam and paved, though narrow—room for one car.

I was curious about Boris, the Russian who I might have asked to camp on his property, so I thought I'd explore Lordville a little. But Lordville seemed to be all Boris. On both sides of the street were odd art installations, unexpected for the river tripper, although somehow in keeping with the tripping the day before.

The first thing I noticed when I crossed the railroad tracks was an old red bus with Herrell's Ice Cream painted in gold lettering on the top, the railing for the sightseeing deck, the words "The Magic Bus" on the body below. And beyond that a house, but with various additions, windows, walls, decks, and landings, a kind of *Swiss Family Robinson* compound with chickens in the yard. Colorful flags—eyes and hearts and other designs—were strung from tree to pole. The mailbox was made from two rocket-like tubes, with USA printed on one, Lordville on the other, a heart on the door to the box. Across the street was a sign for Petticoat Junction, but also a museum to the art and poetry of Konstantin Kuzminsky.

I saw a woman emerge from one of the rooms, cross a balcony, and I wanted to talk to her, find out more. But she had headphones on and held an open laptop. I might have whistled, flagged her over, but it was early, and I was also busy keeping Sully away from the compound's cat. And then the watch-cat, black with a white nose, started to pursue us, or Sully more accurately. Preventing the interspecies brawl led me back down to the river. Besides, I had miles to go before I would sleep, or wake again in the middle of the night.

I would learn later that Kuzminsky was the leader of an underground Soviet nonconformist and Russian émigré troupe of writers and artists in the sixties. He found himself in the underground art scene of New York and later, Lordville. Kostia, as he was called, was a "salty fish from Leningrad who was a sort of soldier on the frontier of the freedom of the human intellect and spirit," Stuart Heady reminisced upon his death in 2015. Even prior to his emigration, he brazenly supported and arranged unofficial apartment exhibitions showcasing alternative art movements, forbidden by the Soviet Union's communist doctrines of the time. He was known to nurture and support some writers (he called his acolytes his "chipmunks") but came into conflict with others, including Joseph Brodsky and Allen Ginsberg. Kuzminsky told the author of "Howl" that his poems were "shit sandwiches."

A larger-than-life personality, "Kostia loved language," wrote Heady, "so he used the sounds from any and all languages in a musical whimsy in his performances. He was a vivid and passionate and completely honest guy. After a night of trading stories and killing off bottles of wine and vodka, I found myself awakening on a bare floor. I couldn't move. I realized that Kostia had me pinned down like a wrestler. His cigarette-drenched beard was in my face. As I focused, he asked me, 'Who are you?'" He meant it not in the intruder sense, but the existential one.

He is survived by his wife Emma "Mouse" Podberyozkina. The historian and author, John E. Bowlt, wrote that in the end, "only one person, his devoted wife, Emma, could withstand and still nurture the vastness of his passionate tantrums, mercurial moods, and almost supernatural artistic stamina. [Kostia] was a product of Mother Russia and he bore high the banner of her culture as he told the world about Russia's literary and artistic wonderland, of which he was both dragon and wizard."

Dragons and wizards, witches on shore—more excitement than I bargained for. But the river was easy going, some riffles with eddies behind. I saw an eagle, and then another. With the Rising Nation group, we tried to keep count but lost track at around thirty. For the first few we spied, someone would let out a *whoop* WOO, and someone in the next boat would echo. Pretty soon, they would break into song. Often this communication seemed nonverbal: just someone looking intently in a tree or at the sky, attuned to each other's perception. An "ooh" or an "ah" would come on, and acknowledgment from someone else. Nature—it amazes everyone.

I stopped in the town of Long Eddy, named for the long pond leading up to it. I walked to the hotel and saloon, but it didn't open until eleven, another twenty minutes, so I walked around some. Next door an old dry goods store had been converted to a baby room design studio. I asked a woman working if this was a good town. "It is. But on Friday night people go crazy." There were barbecue pits and picnic tables behind the saloon. I pictured this as the site of the craziness.

Towns grew up along these eddies to serve the timber rafts, "these rough-and-ready timber sailors," historian Frank Dale writes in *Delaware Diary*. They were places to rest, resupply. Hoff had lunch at the Maple Grove House, which I had seen a plaque for. Cold roast beef, eggs, pickles, applesauce, ice cream, and pie. He was eating better than I was. "It took an hour to do justice to the viands, and the sick ones, sick no longer, performed wonders in the eating line."

They also had a tour of the furnaces where wood was burned and some of the steam, smoke, and gas captured in pipes, condensed, and distilled into an alcohol (methanol, used in varnishes then), or to make tar, or charcoal.

≈ ≈ ≈

The chemical processes recalled those used in hydraulic fracturing, or fracking, which typically involves shooting pressurized water mixed with sand and chemicals—some of which, like methanol, are hazardous to human health—into the shale to crack it open. However, what exact chemicals the industry uses are a mystery, as they are exempt from the Safe Drinking Water Act. When the rock is split open, the gas is captured, like in the processes Hoff describes.

In February 2021, the five-member Delaware River Basin Commission (DRBC), the interstate government agency that oversees the basin, voted 4–0 to permanently ban the extraction of methane gas in the region. The decision came a decade after the commission authorized a moratorium on well construction and followed others on the East Coast, including

New York in 2014, marking a historic win for anti-fracking activists. The DRBC is composed of the governors of New York, New Jersey, Pennsylvania, and Delaware along with the northeastern division head of the US Army Corps of Engineers. The federal appointee abstained. The commission was created sixty years ago to enact unified regulations for the river among members of the four states that share it.

The decision to permanently protect the watershed from fracking was the culmination of years of dedicated activism and public input. The text of the resolution said that fracking "presents risks, vulnerabilities and impacts to surface and groundwater resources in the Delaware River Basin." New York and New Jersey have hardly any natural gas to speak of, but seven Pennsylvania counties within the watershed, including Wayne to my right, sit on Marcellus shale, which holds reserves of natural gas.

When the filmmaker, Josh Fox, whose family used to vacation near here at a cabin on the river, was offered money by a gas company to lease nineteen acres, he gave a "no thanks" and set out to learn more. The resulting 2010 film, *Gasland*, "ignited" controversy, especially because of a scene where a Colorado woman lights a faucet on fire. Methane can occur in taps naturally, but the Pennsylvania Department of Environmental Protection has concluded that shale gas drilling has contaminated hundreds of drinking water wells. Wastewater spills, which can contain heavy metals, have contaminated surface water. Wastewater impoundments have also leaked, leading to groundwater pollution. But not anymore in the watershed. Let's drink to that.

≈ ≈ ≈

From another plaque, I learned that the Long Eddy Hotel was built in the 1850s as a blacksmith shop. Then it became a saloon, the Pig's Foot, for the pickled dainties served at the bar for free. It was likely a stopping place for the rafters bringing their logs downstream. Posters advertised an upcoming fly-fishing festival, Lyme disease symptoms, auto repair, and Vinyasa flow classes.

I heard a woman in a car talking with a Lowe's representative about some kind of appliance repair. Tones of stress as she held, got transferred, no answers to her question. She opened the saloon door and I went in shortly after. The bar was a classic one, a mirror behind with bottles lining the wood shelves. The TVs seemed to come on with the lights. The weary woman sat at a stool with phone in hand. She turned to look at me: "we don't open for ten minutes." I told her I didn't really want anything, that I was on a river trip and wanted to talk, but her attention was elsewhere. Dishwasher. Washing machine. Range.

Back to the boat.

I had about twenty-five more miles to Narrowsburg, so I paddled on, finding a rhythm. Some small streams entered and the river began to take on more volume. We canoed through small riffles with eddies behind, trance-inducing, hypnotic. An eddy is basically recirculating water, a conveyor belt of water moving from the bottom back up toward the obstruction. An eddy is not named after anyone, and may come from Old English, *ed* (turning, back, reverse) and *ea* (water, river). A rock creates a backflow, contrary to the current, and often a safe harbor for downriver boaters. But there can be long eddies too, like the one above Long Eddy and the one I was heading to. Narrowsburg is the deepest place in the river and was once called Big Eddy.

After riffles came small, aerated bubbles, paused in these larger eddies. Where the water deepens it darkens into the color of afternoon tea. I had found a paddling rhythm, but also had plenty of time to contemplate foamy bubbles. Foam rises to the top from white to tan, a froth on a coffee, and is the result of decaying organic matter, which dissolves and becomes active on the surface, a surfactant.

While contemplating foam, I also contemplated the day before and Sherri's question: "was I going through something?" Perhaps there were gender norms at play here. For me, a solo journey down a river seemed no big thing. A quick cyber search for books about "solo adventure" turns up titles of men traveling from Ireland to India by bike, slipping in behind the Great Wall in the early days of communism, and hacking through the jungle in Orinoco. Women might not have the luxury to go for the sake of going, not that there was anything luxurious about my travel. I did not fear camping alone, but I know women who would. For many, to be a woman traveling alone invited peril. The female authors I turned up in the same category often had a big reason to go. Think of Cheryl Strayed hiking the Pacific Crest Trail in *Wild*. Certainly going through something: death of a mother, drug addiction, divorce. In *Heartbreak*, the science journalist, Florence Williams, writes about the science of loss and the benefits of awe. On her canoe voyage of self-discovery after a break with her

husband, Williams notes that the woman-alone-in-the-wilderness narrative is the "next frontier in female power."

To answer Sherri, the truth is I had gone through something. The
stroke led to some serious reexamination, a recirculation of both blood
and thought stream. On a medical leave from teaching that semester
I mostly walked. We had two new dogs on our farm, Sully and one other,
and I walked with them to burn off puppy energy. They wouldn't let me
nap anyway. One day the blue heeler mix wandered off a trail cut through
our marsh, perhaps after a deer. Our property was bounded by brush and
old fencing, but there was a small section of lawn near the neighbors. The
dog had come out there and that's where I found him, lying still by the
side of the road.

A declining marriage is about more than any single event. Admittedly,
I wasn't thrilled about yet another pet to take care of. Just as the nest was
emptying it was being filled, closing off opportunities for travel, exploration. I thought we might be entering the cruise control phase of adult-
hood, the kids grown and flown. I never wanted to hurt the dog, or my
wife. But the dog dying on my walk was perceived that way, bringing
other issues to the surface. It was of a piece with other instances that gave
an impression that she was married to someone who did not respect her
wishes, her boundaries, property or otherwise. That she wasn't loved in a
manner that felt trustworthy. The stroke had caused stress, the dog dying
had, and householding two children for twenty-some years its own kind
of stress. We talked in January. By March, a pandemic added yet more
stress. We might have reversed course, backpaddled, but the current was
too strong. And what was around the bend seemed, at the time, better
than the present stretch.

The long flat periods of a river, the long eddies, with little current or
variation, without even the slightest riffle or wave, lack variety, even joy.
At some point, one has to exit into the faster water and flow. We sold the
farm and parted ways.

After the stroke and separation, and in the early stages of the pandemic, I lived in a cabin on a hill for a while at the corner of Happy
Hollow Road, hoping to find some happiness again, to shake off some
sense of failure. For a long time I felt stuck, as if in the recirculating wave
behind a rock. A flick of the paddle will keep you in there, but another
will flip you back into the current. I didn't want to be married but didn't

want to be unmarried. I wanted my home but not if someone else did not. I missed my familiar walks. Eventually, across the street from the cabin, I discovered a trail down the hill and through the woods, where someone had arranged small, white limestone rocks into crevices at the base of trees, or stacked in little cairns. They lined the path in odd places, sometimes with bits of moss for decoration. It was as if they said look again. It's more beautiful than you thought. More purposeful and deliberate too. And at the bottom of the switchbacked trail, orange chanterelles, and past them, a small creek, and beside it, an old rock hearth and chimney still standing, tied in with lintel stone. Paths to discover, pasts that would remain.

≈ ≈ ≈

Just before Callicoon I came to an island. The map suggested the channel was left, but that way looked too shallow and gravelly. So I veered right. Since 1966, much had changed in both man and map.

The village was quiet. Docks and platforms but no people. On the side of the island, a family was out swimming, so I veered over. I tried out my question: "what brings you to the river?"

"Cooling off," said the father. Splashing, said the kids, without saying. "Too cold for me," said the mother, sitting on the bank.

An older man sat on the bank with a stylish hat. "What brings *you* to the river?"

"The river." Nice one.

"I'm headed to Trenton," I volunteered. See how it sounded day two.

"Enjoy yourself."

I had been trying to catch two kayakers, the first non-motorized boaters I had seen. A tower appeared above the green trees, Romanesque, from the St. Joseph's Seraphic Seminary, I would learn, built in 1904. And above it, on seminary hill, a new cidery.

Bob and Deb, the kayakers, told me so. They asked where I was from, where I was going—same answer for both. Bob was from north Jersey. Why'd he leave?

"It's not saturated here."

Said Deb, "You can pull out of your driveway. More than five cars and you think it's a funeral." She was from the Jersey Shore, and liked the cooler weather, but it would be in the nineties today.

Just downstream, we heard bagpipes, like some expressive aria. But Deb wasn't having it. She was annoyed by the sound.

I cruised on, the man from the morning's words in my head as a song, *Enjoy yourself, it's later than you think.* I had the Specials version, but retired Deb might have had the Doris Day version, the guy on the bank with the hat the Guy Lombardo one.

The river miles go by, as quickly as a wink, at least when there is current. Pretty soon I was past Cochecton, which Hoff told me is a corruption of the name of a Lenape leader and chief during the revolution, Koquethagechton, also known as White Eyes.

The Lenape paddlers played their own songs, a water song I was told, *hey ya hey ya* reverberating off the bank, very often a drum or flute too. Days and weeks later, those songs stayed in my head.

The group camped just below Cochecton at Willow Wisp Organic Farm and Farm Arts Collective. Owners Greg Swartz and Tannis Kowalchuk grow vegetables, herbs, and flowers on twenty-five acres. Tannis also puts on a theater program in one of the converted greenhouses. On a tour, Greg touted the benefits of organic farming and soil health. He also rotated crops, as Natives once did. Shelley had mentioned to me that a good many colonists in the Delaware Valley married Lenape women because they could farm, work the soil. I thought about the centuries of traditional knowledge that went into working the land. Like a plow, colonialism severed Indigenous people from belief systems, their connection to water and land.

Greg and Tannis invited neighbors for a potluck. That night, around the fire and before the drumming, Adam mentioned how he was young for the tribal council, and that they needed to nurture a new generation, mentioned Tamanend and Ahlankw, also Wolf and Coyote, two of the best singers. While they sang, Greg and Tannis's neighbors joined us at the fire, invited us to use their patio and treehouse shower. Chief Chuck gathered the drummers, pulled them in close. "We're going to play an *old* song," Chuck told the audience, and the group started into "She'll Be Coming 'Round the Mountain When She Comes" to howls of laughter. "What? I didn't say it would be an old Indian song." Humor is an old tradition among Indigenous people, a way to cope and heal, a form of resiliency.

Chuck mentioned that there were songs they didn't play for an audience, sacred ones. But then the neighbors, between songs, announced that

that very evening they had become grandparents. "Name him Delaware," someone said. Chuck had the group play an honorary song. Cultural continuity. Unity. Unlike the will-o'-the-wisp, the ghost light or giddy flame (*ignus fatuus*) the traveler sees at night, it did not seem an elusive goal.

≈ ≈

On the first trip, I pulled in on river left just before Skinners Falls where Lander's outfitters had a campground and store. At a beach area, people played more music, not bagpipes but salsa. And many were out in the water, swimming, throwing a soccer ball. I pulled in to rest, tighten life jackets on me and Sully before running the class II rapid.

At the store, Gail told me that last year was an "insane year." Because of Covid restrictions, especially in New York where people could not travel out of state, they came in droves. I bought some ice and she asked where I was headed. When I gave an answer, Will, a young man also behind the counter, said that his father did it once.

"What about you?" I asked.

He shrugged. "Would like to. Someday."

"It's later than you think," I wanted to say/sing.

Skinners Falls is named for one of the first individuals, as legend has it, to float timber from the headwaters to market in Philadelphia. Hoff and crew pulled over to take a look but did not like what they saw. They could not "discover any decided channel in the swiftly rushing torrent." I saw huge boulders, some ledges, and horizontal shale slabs, many with potholes in them, worn by gravel and water. They eased the canoes over, dropping them into eddies with lines attached to both bow and stern. In one spot, they had to carry the loaded canoes over a rock to avoid it. At the bottom, they resolved to "fall over a precipice, should we meet one, rather than make another like 'carry.'" It was the hardest work they did the whole trip.

I had not recently read his description of the rapid or had forgotten it, but I knew of Skinners's reputation. And there was a warning at the bridge: dangerous rapids ahead. It was late in the day and I still had miles ahead of me. I hated taking risks when tired, maybe not making a good decision. Most ski injuries seem to occur on that "one more run," when fatigued and a little careless.

≈ ≈ ≈

People came and went on the Rising Nation journey, but of the thirty or so boats at the beginning of the trip, about five to six were "safety," members of the National Canoe Safety Patrol. People joined the Rising Nation tour because they were Lenape people, or friends of, or had taken Shelley's class, or because they had previously done trips with the Delaware River Sojourn, which goes every year in June. Dave Eagleheart Simon led safety on our trip and works with the National Canoe Safety Patrol. He told me that many people paddle the river not knowing what they're getting into. "They think it will be an easy ride in the park, until they get in trouble." Simon, who worked for twenty-eight years with Bethlehem Steel until it closed in 2003 (two years before full pension), has done every Delaware River Sojourn, every day, every mile since it began. The Sojourn, a multi-day, guided paddle down the river, celebrated its twenty-fifth anniversary in 2019. The Sojourn started as a way to get more people on the river to learn about it and encourage stewardship.

In short presentations throughout the paddle, organizations up and down the watershed talk about why working to protect the watershed is important and why engaged citizens are critical to their success. Kate Schmidt, the Delaware River Basin Commission representative to the Sojourn, told me that "by getting folks of all ages out and experiencing the river firsthand, we hope to educate and create stewards of our shared water resources." Janet Sweeney, director of the northeast region for the Pennsylvania Environmental Council, told the sojourners in her lunchtime presentation that "bringing people to the river makes them love it, and you protect what you love."

Dave and his wife Jane were honored with the Sojourn's inaugural Thousand-Mile Paddler's Award, having completed that many miles. He missed 2020 when it did not run due to Covid concerns, and 2021 because of open-heart surgery. He is the one who told me about the Lenape trip, invited me along. Doing this trip "encouraged me to get better."

At our safety meetings, Dave reminded people about wearing their life jacket, and about what to do if you fall out of your boat. He wore a baseball hat with an eagle patch, the words "Native Pride" on the front, a Vietnam veteran flag on the side. He is tan from miles of river travel, and has a small moustache and a braided ponytail, his "Covid tail." Slight in build, a former marathoner with an arthritic knee, Dave got down on the ground to show us the proper position for feet up if you fall out of your boat. He also mentioned what others might do to help those in the water.

Not drag them into the boat, as that could cause more capsizing, but staying with them, guiding them to shore.

The first day, Dave was paddling a smaller, more nimble boat than his usual Mohawk Shaman. Dave didn't start paddling until his forties, but then he was hooked. This one, also red, had *wanishi*, the Lenape word for "thank you," written on the side. It was a gift from a friend and Dave was trying it out. A few short hours after the safety demo, a wind came up while Dave was looking upstream, watching us navigate a riffle, and flipped him. He was able to stand in the two feet of water, a no-no if the water is really moving (a foot can get wedged) and hold his boat. But everyone converged, grabbing his hat, a water bottle, a few loose pieces of padding he uses for comfort when he kneels.

As much as there were environmental caretaking goals, for this trip and the Sojourn, there seemed to be emotional ones as well, people helping and looking after one another. And yet, the safety could feel like overkill. The guides would cover every small rapid and rock, eliminating hazards. They would choose a safe line to the right, when the more interesting one with wave action and eddy lines was over on river left. For an experienced paddler, it was a little like telling a cook how to chop an onion or boil water. But they had seen things go wrong, very wrong in an instant, and wanted to ensure our safe passage. And I was learning from others on the trip how important was gratitude, for our safety, for the river that took care of us, we of it.

≈ ≈ ≈

I thought I would scout unless an obvious route presented itself, as one did not for Hoff. But by the time I might have pulled over I was entering the swift water. You do a quick visual scan when you "read and run" a rapid. You find a line through rocks, a tongue of smooth water, and a path after that. There are micro-adjustments to make, a flick of the paddle to tilt the boat this way or that. The pulse quickens, the body reacts. A gut drop when you first enter. The water to the left pillowed over large rocks, roiling waves and a gnash of spray, cascading. I stayed right, but then drifted toward the center. Sully had been lying down under the front seat. When she heard the roar of waves, and as the boat rocked and took on a little water, she rose quickly to look at the circumstances. Not liking what she saw, or the splash of water, she wanted to hop into the stern with me, maybe in my arms. But that would rock the boat more, raise our center of gravity. I went to my knees to lower it, yelled "stay" while pivoting between rocks, no eddy or safe harbor to rest in. I could see a dangerous hydraulic to the left I wanted to avoid so I dragged my paddle on the right to swerve the boat away. When we crashed through one last big foamy plume, a woman sitting in the middle on a rock gave us the thumbs-up. In the eddy at the base of the falls I looked back to see what we had come through. A rapid always seems worse at the top, with a drop ahead of you, the unknown, than at the bottom. No big deal you think, having made it, your heart beating fast in your chest, the spit in your throat a little dry.

You always remember the spills. Replay them again and again. The mind churns through the missteps, the what-might-have-beens.

At last, after rounding a bend, what was once Big Eddy, the deepest eddy on the river, now Narrowsburg. The foam flecks swirled in the eddy before the ramp. They narrowed into a circular pattern, reminding me of time-lapse photos of the night sky.

Pulling into Narrowsburg, I had a different song in my head, by the Band, *feeling 'bout half past dead*. I really did just need a place to lay my head. Tired and sore, thirty miles behind me, including a lot of flatwater paddling, I trudged up the boat ramp to pay my campsite fee. Although the ramp was littered with rafts, paddles, life jackets—likely the weekend's spree—I had the large lower area to myself.

Hoff made it over to the Arlington, where Fraulein Gutheil served them with "laughing eyes, pearly teeth, and vivacious manners." Their grace was in the language of Shakespeare: "God comfort thy capacity."

I made pasta with pesto on my camp stove. Restored, I walked around some, hearing that there was ice cream nearby. I caught Nora's Loving Spoonful as they were closing. In fact, they were closed and cleaning up. And I had a card but no cash, and they didn't take cards. I did have one check in case of emergencies, and this was one. I made a check out for $2.67 for a vanilla cone with rainbow sprinkles, jimmies.

A year later I would camp in the exact same spot, with thirty or so people I was getting to know better, along with the river. We sat around the fire and shared some of our motivations for coming. Other people were definitely going through something. We were transitioning, moving, seeking, healing. Something you learn from the river—it is always changing, whether over a year or a day. Life is fluid, and nothing stays the same for very long.

After each person spoke, a new word, *tëmike* (te-MIK-ay), for come in, or welcome. It was a cloudless, starry night, and when we were finished, Adam, the storykeeper and member of the tribal council, told us about the seven sisters, also known as the Pleiades, also known as "the shining collection" to Lenape people.

There were seven wise women elders who the tribe peppered with questions, so many questions they wanted to get away. So they did, and became "standing ones," trees. When trees cooed and whispered, the nation discovered it was them, and they came back with the questions. The standing ones tired of this again, so they retreated farther up the mountain, becoming rocks. One day, out on a hunt, someone tapped one of these, and it made a noise, so the nation came back with their trivial questions. Finally, the women changed again, their rock forms becoming stars, *ahlankw*. No longer would they be pestered with silly questions, or walk among the humans, but would ponder the big, important questions for many moons.

Although the circumstances that brought us there were very different, the journey felt like something we were all in on together, there beneath the stars, the paths of planets, the same celestial events above whether watching or not.

A year before, I walked back to camp through the trees sifting the night. The air was still warm, even at nightfall. Then, I had yet another song in my head, the Lovin' Spoonful's "Daydream," even though it was night. What a night for it. The trees were saturated with shadow. I had come a long way. In the flyless tent, the moon and stars, the whole shining collection appearing to hang motionless over the still water, this boy dreamed.

The Narrowsburg-Darbytown bridge, built in 1954.

RAPIDS

Day 3—Narrowsburg to Shohola
290–272

I woke to a quiet rain dripping through the mesh. With sore shoulders and bare feet, I stretched on the fly and burrowed back in my bag, waiting out the droplets. When the patter stopped, I connected a canister to the stove and heated water for coffee in a stainless-steel French press. I once broke a glass one while pressing and was so desperate for coffee I was willing to extract the shards from the grounds in the base of the carafe, salvage the nectar. When I told a friend about this, the metal one arrived at the door.

Phone service told me about the ice cream last night and nearby, even more coffee. I had a full mug but was up for a walk before a full day on the river.

I made my way back over the tracks, past Nora's, noting what I missed last night outside the glare of my headlamp. At 2 Queens Coffee I ordered an espresso and a blueberry scone, as much for the chance to chat as to eat or drink.

It was going to be a hot day, and one of the owners, Martin, told me he would be swimming under the bridge later. His suit was ready. I told him where I was headed, and he told me I was "going the distance," so now I had another song in my head, by Cake.

Later outside on the patio, I learned the story of the name from the other co-owner, Charles. He liked bees, but it was a nod to the other kind of "queen." They strive to be inclusive and sustainable: "98 percent of people don't care. Those that do, we don't want them here anyway."

Until recently, I rarely gave my privileged status as a straight male much consideration. The 2016 shooting at the gay nightclub Pulse in Orlando prompted me to rethink it, as did the 2022 shooting at Club Q in Colorado Springs. I rarely go anywhere and feel threatened for who I am or am with. No one has ever refused me a wedding cake or a morning scone. But my daughter might have been in that club with her friends, or my son with his. Within their social settings, they and their friends are mostly welcomed if they identify as queer or straight. Their generation has grown up without the stigma over same-sex attraction and partnering, but they have also known the hateful violence that others have directed at them, including an increasing hostility among state legislatures toward gender expression.

One group on the Rising Nation trip arrived late from the drive to Philadelphia. They pitched their tent in the dark on the asphalt parking lot. In the morning, the three of them piled gear into a rented Grumman that would keep getting stuck. It would have hung up more if the ground crew had not taken their gear. Two were a couple and at least one gender nonconforming, but they were welcomed by Chief Chuck Gentlemoon himself. Shelley mentioned that some Indigenous people were "two-spirit," both hunters and gatherers. Some tribes assigned roles, but some did both, or oscillated between one or the other, "and they were revered." Enx Eeeden—herbalist, body artist, and teacher—was also on the trip. They had published the book *Nonbinary Healing Practices across the Globe*.

The café served a lot of weekenders from the city, but at the moment, the only other customer was a local construction business owner who couldn't find help. At Pete's Market next door, I picked up some turkey and pickles for lunch, and replenished my beer supply, a Devil's Path IPA from Catskill Brewery.

Back at camp, I caught up with Rick Lander, the owner of the camp-ground and Lander's River Trips. I asked about what Gail told me yester-day, their record year last year.

The Skinners Falls beach, he told me, was their Jones Beach. Because all the water parks were closed, Hershey Park closed, people came here. New York had strict regulations about leaving the state, but he was in-state, and families couldn't gather inside, but they could get ten relatives and a few campsites and get together around a campfire. Just two hours from the city.

His father Bob from Brooklyn started the business. He used to go to Ten Mile Scout Camp as a boy and later worked there summers. In 1955 he bought Ten Mile River Motel and turned it into a rustic lodge. With just ten canoes, he began renting and running trips on the river. Son Rick has grown the business to eight launch sites, three campgrounds, a restau-rant, and a gas station.

Rick claims that they were there first. Kittatinny, the other main outfit-ter, "had two Jon boats behind a bar." Lander has seen many changes to the industry, from canoes to kayaks to rafts. The rafts are more social, and you don't flip. Too, some of the conflicts, the "divorce machines" as they can be known, when couples disagree on which way to navigate obstacles, can be minimized.

The hierarchy on a ship ensures smooth operation and coordination in case decisions need to be made. The "two-spirit" boaters from Phila-delphia developed a system they called "fluidly hierarchical." Mercie, in the stern, had the most experience, so they steered, while Carrie sat in the middle and Kio paddled from the bow. They kept getting hung up, so the system kept adapting: better communication, a "power" left to differenti-ate from a regular left stroke. And when they hit, was it the lookout's fault or the steerer? We can all use a little mercy.

Lander now serves a different customer. "We used to serve a lot of hunters. And I could probably name thirty to forty that built houses up here." Now, he described a lot of younger folks tethered to technology. How he advertises has changed, from traditional media to "influencers," which he was still wrapping his head around.

His customers still came from Brooklyn, like his father, but they are Central American, Eastern European. And as many as they had last year, a hundred or more years ago people also flocked to the area. Then, as now, a disease ran people out of the city. One recommended cure for highly infectious tuberculosis was fresh air.

TB, like Covid, attacked the lungs, and people were told to "go to the mountains." Nearby, Gilded Age financier J. P. Morgan, whose first wife died of TB three months after their wedding, donated $85,000 (nearly 3 million today) to build the Loomis Sanitarium. The 192-acre sanitarium village opened in 1901 and included twenty buildings in a blend of commune and medical center. Named after Alfred Loomis, a physician and patient, the facility combined components of traditional Western medicine with those of homeopathy. This integrative approach resulted in groundbreaking diagnosis and treatment protocols still practiced today. X-rays and laboratory tests were first used in TB diagnoses, and the link between victims and consumption of unpasteurized milk from TB-infected cows was recognized.

The sanitariums were early experiments in quarantine, and Loomis pioneered the concept of "auto-inoculation," later the field of immunotherapy, the idea that the best defense against disease is a strong offense mounted by the body's own immune system. Vaccines would be based on it. Loomis based the treatment on his personal experience living in the mountains, and auto-inoculation was thought to be a by-product of fresh air, clean water, regular exercise, and healthy food. Loomis's patients grew much of their own food, did mental and physical work as illness permitted, slept outdoors, either on porches or in lean-tos or tents, and stimulated their immune systems with herbs.

According to a pamphlet, the sanitarium offered "climatic advantages": "The elevation is within those limits generally conceded to be most favorable for the climatic treatment of diseases of the throat and lungs." It was free of humidity and fog. "Hopeless cases," however, were not admitted.

Rick Lander was on the board of the local hospital, and he swore they didn't have any Covid cases at the time.

In the mid-1950s, when Rick's father started the business, there were 538 hotels, 1,000 boarding houses, and 50,000 bungalows in all of Sullivan County. Postwar mobility and the polio vaccine had Americans on the move. In the summer of 1952, every single hotel room and bungalow was booked for the entire summer. According to Sullivan County historian

John Conway, by some estimates up to 2.5 million visitors came to Sullivan County and its "borscht belt" resorts in the peak years of 1955–1965.

≈ ≈ ≈

There are no signs of such activity now, just a sleepy hamlet with an impressive arch-span bridge. The river here is over a hundred feet deep and with houses perched above on the rocky shore, the scene reminded me of Maine.

In the deep water, I pulled my paddle through the foam-flecked river and pointed Margaret downstream. An eagle made a move on the rocky outcrop, dropping a feather that I steered over for and reached to pick up. I stuck it in the seat back behind me.

I had a big day ahead, with some twenty-five rapids in front of me, including Ten-Mile, West Colang, Narrows Falls, Big Cedar, and Shohola— all class IIs. This section of the river would descend over a series of bedrock ledges through the Appalachian Plateau.

At the start of it, yet more eagles. It seemed like I could get closer to the juvenile ones, almost near their perch. The "bald" in the eagle comes from an older meaning of bald, "streaked with white," as in piebald. The white-headed adults hid in the tops of trees or took flight when I approached. But sometimes the juveniles, mottled brown and white, would wait until I was just upon them before fleeing a perch. Several times, I saw what looked to be a parent come by to screech at the youngster, chase it in flight, as if to say "what were you thinking? Letting that human get so close?" Or so it seemed, as if it were some kind of training.

This had me thinking about whether young eagles were like young people, their reward system overtaking their impulse control. A love of the new and novel leads directly to useful experience, and possible reward. That same hunt for sensation provides the inspiration needed to get out of the house, or nest. Taking a risk meant that young eagle found a new section of river to inhabit, like its parent before. Long ago, an eagle took a chance on the river itself, flying up from the Delaware Bay.

Last summer on a kayaking trip to the Chattooga, the famous river where *Deliverance* was filmed, I dropped over a class IV ledge and started to flip at the bottom. I braced on the leaning side, the upriver side, ready to roll if I had to, but also trying to prevent turning upside down. My paddle jammed into a rock below, the kayak drifting downstream, increasing my arm angle, and my shoulder slipped out of joint. When it gave, I pulled the skirt and ejected, felt not so much pain as lack of function, and swam toward shore with the good arm. On a rock, the shoulder seemed to wind back into the socket. I emptied my boat of water, adrenaline shaking my knees. I thought I was fine—no big deal. But several hundred yards later, the tissue now weakened, it happened again in a small wave, just paddling. This time it was even more painful. Luckily, we were near a ramp, and not far from the put-in. So, with the help of a friend, we walked back to the trucks at the put-in and found ice for the shoulder.

A year later, the joint felt pretty good, near full strength. And a canoe paddle angle is lower than a kayak one. But I wondered what would happen if I did need help. The stroke was always in the back of my mind too. I wondered about my ability to misread the warnings, the severity of what lay ahead, or if I would overestimate my skill. From what I had read, everything downriver was class II, meaning waves and some obstruction, but pay attention and I should be fine.

My sixties map had its own scale from I to VI, with six representing simply hazardous and "swift flowing." Someone might think that if they completed a III on the Delaware, "riffle," they could on any river.

That series of maps was eventually upgraded according to the international scale of river difficulty, created by the American Canoe Association. Whitewater is basically air trapped in the water, making it appear opaque or white, usually the result of gradient or change in flow. The system rates an individual rapid (or a stretch of river) according to six categories from class I (easiest and safest) to class VI (most difficult and most dangerous). The grade reflects both the technical difficulty and the danger associated with a rapid. The higher the class, the bigger the drop and the bigger the "consequences." With class III and above, they should likely be scouted or known in advance. With class IV, there are very often "must make" moves.

There was risk involved in coming on this trip, the many rapids to cross, but there was risk in not coming too, the regrets I might have. Know what else is risky? Going just about anywhere, any day. And it's especially risky to stay at home, being a vessel of the expectations of others.

≈ ≈ ≈

At a boat ramp to take a break, I saw another canoe loaded with camping gear, the only other one I had encountered. Andrea, husband Braden, and teenage son Tucker, in a kayak, were waiting for their brother/uncle and his kids, taking a lunch break in the shade. Andrea's father worked for Kittatinny, the other main outfitter on the river, and he used to take them on trips. This was their annual one.

Andrea's father became a canoe instructor and trained in swift water (or whitewater) rescue. Such training uses ropes and mechanical devices (such as hauling systems) to deflect the water's power and allow rescuers to reach an endangered person. Flowing water is deceptively strong, often trapping unwary persons. Her father, Kirk, kept a clicker of the rescues they performed. They performed over 1,500 rescues in the 1980s.

Midday, it was hard to find shade on the river. Another day above ninety degrees. Narrowsburg saw five days above ninety the year I was born, 1966. Today, twice that. And by the end of the century, about twenty days.

I fell into a pattern of paddle, sunscreen, drip a little water on Sully with paddle, dip hat in water, paddle, sunscreen.

We passed Masthope Creek and the village of Masthope, derived from a Lenape or Algonquin term for glass beads, although legend has it that this area was the "last hope" for the main mast of the *USS Constitution*, "Old Ironsides." Much of the timber in the region would have been used in Philadelphia shipbuilding, but not likely the 104-foot-tall *Constitution* mast.

People cooled off in the water. "You look relaxed," I said to one man, sitting in the water with his family.

"Bout time—been chores up until this point."

I came to one of Kittatinny's launch areas, where they had a "borrow a life jacket" station—borrow a life jacket as you would a book. A family had discovered a water snake, and a man in a Yankees hat pursued it. "It's harmless," I said, "just a water snake," but it appeared he didn't hear me, or understand my English. But I think the snake made its escape.

≈ ≈ ≈

Chasing the snakes reminded me of those we kids would sometimes find (and avoid) in our swimming hole. We would also, occasionally, catch an eel on our fishing rod. They were hard to remove from a hook, with a slimy mucous coating hard to grab. And they wriggled and coiled around your line. Sometimes we would cut the line. I had no idea, at the time, of their value as a food source to Natives on the Delaware, or of their mysterious origins.

I passed a weir earlier in the day. Eels are catadromous, meaning they are born in salt water and return there to spawn, but they spend their lives in fresh. They are the only North American fish to do this. On their return to the sea, they can be trapped in V-shaped weirs, funnels usually made from rock. Such walls can create significant rapids or rifts. Hoff went over one accidentally, and one of his crew swamped. The one I had seen earlier pushed canoe traffic to the left or right, eels through the center. In the center was usually a net, and now also something like a wooden rack. Though I saw several with wooden structures, still in operation, many more were likely long out of use, barely detectable.

In 1874, a German biologist, Max Schultze, lying on his deathbed, observed that he was leaving a world where "all the important questions" had been settled. Among them—the mysteries of evolution, genetics, chemistry, pasteurization, and vaccination. All of them, that is, "except the eel question." Where did they come from? How were they born?

The Egyptians believed that eels were produced by the sun warming the Nile. For Aristotle eels emerged spontaneously from mud and rainwater. Pliny the Elder had it that new eels developed when old eels rubbed away parts of their bodies on rocks. As late as the 1860s, a Scottish author believed that they began their lives as beetles. "Some believed eels were born of sea-foam," Patrik Svensson writes, in *The Book of Eels*, "or created when the rays of the sun fell on a certain kind of dew that covered lake-shores and riverbanks in the spring." In the English countryside, where eel fishing was popular, most people thought "eels were born when hairs from horses' tails fell into the water."

Two years after Schultze died, a young man of nineteen bought eels from a Trieste fisherman and carried them home to a dissection table in a corner of his room. From morning until night, breaking only for lunch, he cut in search of eel genitalia. "My hands are stained by the white and red blood of the sea creatures," he wrote to a friend. "All I see when I close my eyes is the shimmering dead tissue, which haunts my dreams, and all I can think about are the big questions, the ones that go hand in hand with testicles and ovaries—the universal, pivotal questions." That man would later be consumed by other "big" questions, but then it was eel genitalia. His name was Sigmund Freud.

Johannes Schmidt, a Dane, became so consumed by the question of where they came from that in 1904 he left his family in Copenhagen and scoured the seas for seven years for the smallest of eels. For another three years, he enlisted shipping companies to net larvae as they plied the North Atlantic and turned his own ship west and south. Net by net, he mapped the ocean according to which parts of it contained eel larvae, and how large those larvae were, until the tiniest ones led him to their point of origin. It was a slow process, made slower by a shipwreck and a world war. Finally, nearly twenty years after he first left, Schmidt announced his findings. "How long the journey lasts we cannot say," he wrote, "but we know now the destination sought: a certain area situated in the western Atlantic," near the West Indies. "Here lie the breeding grounds of the eel."

Schmidt had traced the European eel to the Sargasso Sea, a garden of seaweed bounded not by land but by great swirling currents of water. The American eel breeds there as well, and it is still something of a mystery how the larvae, all mixed together but genetically distinct, know which continent is their future home.

They are a creature of metamorphosis, beginning as transparent larva with huge eyes, like a gossamer willow leaf floating in the open sea. Then they become a glass eel, just a transparent sliver a few inches long, with the insides visible like jellyfish. As elvers, they develop pigmentation, and make their way up coasts and rivers. The yellow-brown eel, the kind you might catch in ponds, can move across dry land (absorbing oxygen through gill and skin), hibernate in mud, and live quietly for thirty years in a single place. Finally, the silver eel, nearly two feet long, a powerful tube that ripples its way back to sea. During this last change, the eel's stomach dissolves—it will travel thousands of miles on its fat reserves alone—and its reproductive organs develop for the first time. Freud couldn't find the man or lady parts because they hadn't developed yet. The female will produce millions of eggs, but they die after they spawn.

Expeditions have followed Schmidt to the breeding grounds over the years, with better and better technology. Scientists have tracked silver eels beginning their migration with GPS. They have tried hormones to bring females into heat, transported them to the breeding grounds, and attached them to buoys to use their pheromones as bait. They have dropped microphones into the water and opened the stomachs of predators. And yet no one has ever seen eels mating anywhere, or so much as set eyes on a mature eel, living or dead, in the Sargasso Sea.

Rachel Carson kept a tank of eels in her office and made an eel named Anguilla (the scientific name of eels) a protagonist of her first book, *Under the Sea Wind*. Anguilla lived in the warm mud of a pond, "beyond all reminders of the sea." One day, she felt the urge to depart her current life and to transform and make her way through "frigid waters, deliberate and inexorable as time itself," to a place where no one could follow. "No one can trace the path of the eels," Carson wrote.

While we now know where they go, the most urgent "eel question" at the moment for Svensson: Why are they disappearing?

There are many possible reasons, from disease to dams and locks, from fishing pressure to the warming climate, which is causing the ocean currents by which eels make their migrations to shift and change. But for the most part, they still return and thrive in the Delaware, unlike in nearby rivers, such as the Susquehanna, which is dammed.

The racks harvest eels for food, which is sold to several ethnic groups. They do not successfully reproduce in captivity. As a result, the aquaculture industry that exists in Asia is dependent upon an annual supply of wild-caught glass eels and elvers, another reason for their decline.

Ray Turner, seventy-three, still operates Delaware River Delicacies in Hancock. He has a commercial license to trap and smoke eels, shad, and trout. Turner lives a mostly solitary life, doesn't use a cell phone or answer the landline, "you have to walk in the door and get lucky." His father learned the art from Charlie Howard, who died in 1948. Then, the local paper ran the front-page headline, "Hancock Recluse Lived in Lonely River Cabin." The obituary described Howard as being "as close to the popular idea of a hermit as was Thoreau." He "conducted an eel rack near his home, gaining part of his sustenance from the eels."

For his part, Turner is considering retiring. Imagine "assembling a two-car garage in the middle of the river and having to take it apart every year," he told *New York Upstate*, referring to his eel rack. He also must stand in the river and repair the rock wall leading up to it. But for now, business was good. When I was there in August of 2021, he told me that "people came here from Belarus, Venezuela, Indonesia, Eastern Europe—and some Irish men, too. I've had customers from Australia."

I caught him a year later, and he had just had someone in the store from Greece. They caught something about his shop on one of the ferries, traveled to the end of his dirt road on the East Branch. Ray had me wash up—"your mom would be proud"—and don a mask. Inside, he wore one as well, a blue mask pressing down a long, white beard.

The case had no more eel, because "geezerdom" had caught up with him. But he was glad to sell me some salmon, imported from Scotland and smoked and packaged on site. His packages say, "Ray Turner, gourmet consultant," which is not entirely facetious. In addition to his deli case, he sold locally produced honey, sauerkraut, sweet pickled relish, pickled beets, vanilla peaches, brandied cherries, and a gourmet brand of mustard.

I asked what I should take on the river, and he recommended some cold smoked salmon, like lox, a hunk of New York cheddar to go with, and a sleeve of Ritz crackers, the latter sold for a dollar fifty.

After I paid him, and walked out, he closed the door of his shop, threw up his hands, "whew."

"Friday night," I said.

"Means nothing to me. Maybe the Yankees game," he added.

He wanted to make sure I had enough ice though and gave a lecture on the temperature of a refrigerator, on the ravages of botulism. Neither it, nor Covid, was going to touch Ray.

≈ ≈ ≈

Another group had arrived on a bus, likely from the city. A few men had the side curls of Hasidic Jews. They played loud music. Performing my journalistic duty, I asked where they were from.

"We're from the camp."

"Are you part of the same community?"

"Yes."

"What community is that?"

"The camp community."

I wasn't getting anywhere, but it wouldn't be the last time on the river a group would rather not reveal their ethnic identity. They were Americans, or simply from the summer camp, like everyone else. Or like eels, wishing to conceal their origins.

It was nearing lunch time, and I hoped one of the towns, Lackawaxen on the Pennsylvania side, or Minisink Ford in New York, had a place to stop, rest, and eat. Minisink Ford was the site of a battle during the American Revolution, where forty to fifty settlers were killed by loyalists and Iroquois fighters led by Mohawk chief Joseph Brant. Lackawaxen was home to author Zane Grey, who wrote books about cowboys. It seemed an unlikely place to inspire legends of the Old West, but Grey, a dentist, wrote his 111 books here, including *Riders of the Purple Sage* and *The Lone Star Ranger*. Grey's clapboard home is now maintained as a museum by the Park Service.

Lackawaxen is also famous for its bridge. The bridge is suspended, like the Golden Gate and Brooklyn Bridges, and the oldest of its kind in America, built by Trenton's John Roebling in 1849. The massive stone pillars seem overkill, until you learn that the bridge held not people but water. The Delaware and Hudson Canal, built in 1829, needed a reliable crossing when water was high or ice floes too great. Conventional construction would have required five piers, but a suspension needed only three, leaving room for timber rafts beneath. The channel the bridge supported, the canal above water, was six feet deep and twenty feet wide. The railroad eventually made canal transport unprofitable, but barges loaded with coal or other goods routinely crossed until 1898. It's now a national historic landmark.

When Hoff came through in the 1890s, there was a dam to feed the canal. This dam, sixteen feet high, "constructed in the most approved scientific manner, to secure strength, sluiced the river through a narrow chute on river right, dropping eight feet into huge haystack waves."

Hoff lunched at the Delaware House, and I had hopes for similar fare. At this point in the trip, I had developed two rules: respect the power of the river and base the decision on which town to visit, left or right, New York or Pennsylvania, on which had the easier access to shore. Just above Lackawaxen, a group was in the water drinking beer and playing "Lonesome Cowboy Bill" by the Velvet Underground. Augury was saying the Zane Grey side.

Right it was. The New Inn at Lackawaxen, just past the bridge, had a good place to land and stone steps up to a patio and deck. I walked past the tall shirtless guy mowing with headphones, headed toward the umbrella-ed oasis that seemed a tiki bar. But there was no one sitting there. No umbrellas on either patio or in drinks. I climbed the steps to go inside. Two guys in their chef whites opened the door, startled by Sully and me.

They were closed.

Maybe the Zane Grey Museum after all? At least a shade break. But it was closed as well.

I pouted at the picnic table painted lime green on a lower patio. On it, someone had painted the words Key Largo. Florida imposed on northeastern Pennsylvania. One order stamped on another. You're supposed to feel happy in such settings. An everlasting Margaritaville party. I thought of pulling a beer from the cooler but mostly I wanted cool water, so I asked the college-aged guy mowing the lawn.

He pointed me toward a glowing lawn ornament at the back of the structure, where a spigot dispensed cool water. I wondered if I should lay my hands on the orb in worship. The water was so cold and clear, the sun so hot, I did want to show gratitude for this spring.

On the way out, I thanked Noah, taking a break from the mowing to wipe sweat from his brow and drink his own water. He sported a turtle tattoo on his arm, some Indigenous art. Noah saw a sea turtle while surfing in California once, and it moved him, I could tell. I told him about my own encounter on Georgia's Cumberland Island, a big loggerhead emerging from the depths of the inky sea. About that tattoo, he said, "I'm into the tribal stuff." In the Lenape origin story, North America is known as Turtle Island, formed when a giant turtle rose from the ocean.

Lackawaxen is a Lenape name for "swift waters." The people who created this origin story oriented their lives around rivers. They lived on the riverbanks and also on the islands. The islands rose out of the water like the backs of turtles, climbing out on a stone from the depths. The islands might offer protection, like a turtle's shell, and on them, as on the banks, was a rich floodplain good for planting, and plenty of places to hunt and fish. Bands of both Algonquian-speaking Lenape and Iroquoian-speaking Seneca lived in the area through the early nineteenth century, yet neither tribe had any substantial villages in the area, as they used it for temporary hunting and fishing grounds.

I was merely seeking a place of rest, or repast, and in doing so was thinking of the settlement patterns of Natives versus those of Euro-Americans. Historian Ted Steinberg documents in *Gotham Unbound* how the Dutch West India company instructed a director to round up the New Netherland colonists into one main settlement, a hub for their trading network. They were to choose a place where "the river is narrow, where it cannot be fired upon from higher ground, where ships cannot come too close, where there is a distant view unobstructed by trees and hills, where it is possible to have water in the moat, and where there is not sand, but clay or other firm earth." They suggested three spots: an island not far from Trenton, what is now Jersey City, and the "hook of the Manattes."

The Dutch purchased the island of Manhattan in 1626 for sixty guilders, or a little over a thousand dollars today. The Lenape may have had little choice if they wanted some reciprocal relationship with the settlers, but the real issue may be the different systems for organizing and valuing the land. As best as historians can tell, the idea of selling the land likely never occurred to Indigenous people. Dutch settler Adriaen van der Donck wrote in his *Description of New Netherland* about their belief in collective stewardship. To the Indians, "wind, stream, bush, field, sea, beach, and riverside are open and free to everyone of every nation with which the Indians are not embroiled in open conflict." In "The Selling of Lenapehoking," archaeologist Robert Grumet found that the Lenape practiced a form of land tenure founded on temporary usufructuary rights rather than permanent title, on mutual rights to harvest bounty rather than private property, which turns land into a commodity.

I was glad that at least the water was free to everyone. And to be back on the river, in a space of mutual rights. I am reluctant to "go native," adopt the symbols or iconography of an Indigenous culture, or ink them on my arm. Many people on the Lenape river journey had tattoos, piercings, or ear hoops. In representations, so does Chief Tamanend. Like Noah, we all want to be part of some tribe, and believe in a place or home we can belong to, or at least one we can carry with us.

A year later, on the grounds of the Zane Grey Museum, I watched the Lenape Nation arrange a treaty signing with the Delaware Highlands Conservancy and the Lake Wallenpaupack Historical Society. Shelley and Adam DePaul talked to the audience about the prophecy of the four crows. It was an odd location, since it was one birthplace of the western, the genre in which the white cowboys were heroic and the Indians savage, if noble, often silent.

According to the prophecy, the first crow flew in the way of harmony with creator. The second crow tried to clean the world, but it became sick and died. The third crow saw his dead brother and he hid. The fourth crow flew the way of harmony again with creator. As the Lenape people interpret the story, and conceive of history, it relates the ways in which they have struggled to survive and to keep their community and culture intact. The first crow was the Lenape before the coming of the Europeans. The second crow symbolized the death and destruction of their culture— smallpox, alcohol, persecution, exile. The third crow was their people going underground and hiding. The fourth crow was the Lenape becoming caretakers again, working with everybody to restore the land. They believed that the first river trip signaled the time of the fourth crow.

≈ ≈ ≈

A tailwind improved my morale, and we met more swimmers. A dog swam out to greet us, and the owner just said, "slice of heaven." I had high hopes for another stop near Barryville, the Cedar Rapids Inn, which my eighties guidebook said hosted bluegrass jams and clambakes, but they were mirages I was now conjuring in the heat.

Near the Shohola bridge I passed a giant green party raft, about twenty people and a lot of black T-shirts, but not a lot of sobriety. They wanted to commandeer my beer. But Shohola is a Lenape term for "place of peace," so we coexisted. Coming up, my second late-in-the-day rapid, this time Shohola Rift.

Rapids are basically water and pressure over rocks, ones you white knuckle your way through. Your heart speeds up a little, especially when you can't see over the drop. I stood in the canoe for a minute to scout, and instantly had a plan. Scoot left, then back to right, follow the channel, try not to be mesmerized by the high rocks on the left side. I just missed a giant pour-over in the middle, and at the base, noted a pretty good campsite on river right with a view of the bluffs, called Little Hawk's Nest.

It was still hot, although after six, so I took a delicious swim in the current below the rift. I opened my eyes underwater to look for small minnows, the occasional bass, darting away or holding fast in the current. Some wriggled their whole bodies, some used their caudal or tail fins like rudders, as I did with my paddle.

While opening my eyes underwater, I could see Sully's paddling paws coming near. She has competing instincts when swimming: an urge to join me with a fear of moving water, simultaneously viewing me as life raft and drowning threat. She swam close to check on me and then escaped to the safe shore.

While we both dripped dry, I swept out some of the river cobble with my paddle to make a tent site, like a dog scratching out and circling its bed. Where to sleep is an old argument among river·trippers: sandy beach or pebbly one? One soft but sand everywhere, the other hard but relatively clean.

I smoothed out a pad as best I could and then sat on my stool, tall hemlocks behind, view of high bluffs, soothing river sound. I picked up a few stones and tumbled them in my hand like those Chinese Baoding (meditation) balls, staring at the starry flecks, the streams of white. Gritty smooth like eggshells. Never mind the world in a grain of sand. Here, it's in a handful of rocks.

I started a fire as Andrea and her family came through the rapid. Her brother had arrived and he was out in front. "She said there was a guy with a dog going all the way to Trenton."

"That's me."

Andrea: "Hi Rick!"

All: "Good trip."

I slid a premade foil packet on the embers. Potatoes and carrots and other mixed veggies. I sat on my chair in the river cobble, dug my feet into the stones, waited for the sizzle. The meal came out of the embers steaming, and I half blew on, half inhaled the feast. Sully took great pleasure in licking the charred bits in the discarded foil clean.

Here was reason enough to come: the contrasts of wet and dry, soft and hard, to watch the flames crackle and leap and glow as darkness moved in, the cliff walls across the river already steeped in shadow. The fire smoked and smoldered into ash as the river rushed past, hard and clean and full of force.

The Barryville-Shohola Bridge, built in 2007.

ISLANDS

Day 4—Shohola to Milford

272–245

The energetic chatter of birds in the trees behind me alerted me of the morning. Sully slept while I made my way to my three-legged stool.

In the quiet morning I looked out over the misty river. My torso felt a little stiff, and I had a strange sensation that I was still on the river, paddling, though I sat in stillness on the shore. The torsional act of paddling, and the river twisting, were somehow one and the same. Watching the morning brighten, I recalled hearing nighttime noises, an owl probably, but also, in a dream or half-sleep, the sounds of water moving and shifting the rock. Or it was visiting footsteps touching the gravel around me. And then there was the ghostly swaying of trees on the steep hill behind the tent. It occurred to me that if I sat here listening long enough, I would hear the deep bellows of tumbling boulders scouring the riverbed.

Like last night, I selected a few cobbles to clack in my hand. Time and water smooths stones. As if I could rewind then fast-forward, I envisioned the rises and falls of the river, along with terrestrial visits from protective forest to sip at exposed shore, and avian flights from canopy on down. Like those it harbored, the river was an animal.

I walked on the shore as if to verify the vision, listening to my own footfalls on silt and stone. A few small bird tracks appeared, tiny star prints, and the three-toed marks of a great blue heron. Like a heron stalking, I prowled for other signs, seeing a canine print slightly larger than Sully's, possibly coyote. Last night's disturbance? Farther on, I saw some droppings and the hind feet of a rabbit. Maybe what I heard was predator on prey, exposed out here under the piercing starlight.

Once, near the creek we lived on, I came upon a large sweeping in the snow, tiny flecks of cherry red. It was probably an owl, angel wings hardly angelic—swooping in for the silent kill. I tiptoed around respectfully, as if in the presence of an ancient artifact on display. Walking on the river's margin, I thought of those Tibetan Buddhist mandalas made of colored sand that are then swept away.

Thinking about the ebb and flow of rivers, the visits to and from of animals, the late Barry Lopez writes in *River Notes* that "to stick your hand into the river is to feel the cords that bind the earth together in one piece."

I took down my tent like one of those mandalas. Deflated my sleeping pad, one big exhale. By day four, I had a pretty good handle on the routine of put up and take down. Sully was normally up with me, but I had to roust her. She had probably missed some crucial nap time yesterday, keeping alert. Or was alerted last night by visitors. Soon she was up and on their scent. I marked this camp as one to return to.

After a short morning paddle, the best time to make up some time—before the direct sun—I caught up with Andrea and her brother Scott. While I had made a campsite in the river cobble, they had reserved one. Rather than stay in an Airbnb, they had asked an owner if they could pay to camp on his land.

The owner said sure, only he hadn't mentioned the rooster, so they had been up early. They invited me up for coffee and blueberry pancakes.

I joined them around the campfire, and they told me a little more about their father and their canoe trips when young.

Andrea said those trips were among her "happiest memories." "Maybe my only memories?" she added.

With their father, who worked at Kittatinny Canoes, Scott participated in some of the cleanups the company put on. He remembered finding a fridge missing a door, and first trying to float and paddle it, then laying it precariously across the gunwales of a canoe, steering it to a boat ramp. He races canoes and not refrigerators now.

On their epic cross-country canoe paddle in 1971, seven thousand miles from Montreal to the Bering Sea through old fur-trading routes, canoe legend Verlan Kruger and partner Craig Waddell subsisted mainly on pancakes and calculated that one pancake fueled four miles. I had four pancakes.

We sat around the fire a little, talking of canoes and canoe trips. The fire then, and last night, chased away the chill some, though it was plenty warm. Something about a fire provides feelings of comfort, prevents feelings of longing. Jim Beer, who had the idea for the Rising Nation journey, reminded me that "at one time, all our ancestors gathered around a fire, hunted or gathered food."

I pushed off as they were starting to pack up. I could sense some tension in the group building over who was to do what while they were behind schedule. The dogs chased each other over and through camp, adding to the unease.

When I told people about this trip, many asked the same thing. By yourself? If I had gone a year earlier, my son Sam would have come with me, but he had graduated school in wildlife conservation and had some summer fieldwork lined up. Other friends were maybes, possibly for a stretch, but I didn't know if I wanted to hew to someone else's schedule anyway, to the group dynamics and assigned roles. What I found in paddling with a group is that indeed, there was always someone to talk to. And there was comfort in knowing others were there should something go wrong. But there was also limited down time. And very often I wanted to stop and swim, but the group had a place to get to. Too, our campsites had to be big, often commercial, so the nature experience could be diminished.

When traveling by myself, I tried to notice every merganser, heron, kingfisher, and eagle in a way that felt almost communicative on some silent, prelinguistic level. It felt calming, meditative, to scan the banks and really look and know that they too, in their awareness, were looking back, even if not directly. With the group, I was more attentive to them: to not bumping into boats, learning names, making small talk. But eventually, the group came together in ways I haven't experienced on other river trips.

I was hesitant to join the Lenape trip. Did I belong? Was I an interloper? I heard about it late in the summer, so I scrambled to gather my gear and rearrange my schedule, arrange a shuttle for my car. No dogs were allowed, so I needed a sitter for Sully. Their itinerary said they would camp, so I loaded up, ready to be self-supporting again. Only each night they ran shuttles back to cars, while I stayed behind. I was one of the only boats carrying my gear, and I was one of two or three canoes among thirty boats. Most were in kayaks. I can be shy in groups, reserved. My voice does not seem to carry loudly enough to gain attention. One person even paddled over to me, "I see you over here, keeping to yourself." But I was listening, to them and to the river. And eventually, as I became more comfortable with people on the trip, we seemed to come together as a cohesive whole. Like we were attending to the river together.

Why? It might have been the physical aspect of paddling. I went on a guided trip with strangers who bonded some over the beautiful scenery, but we rarely rowed. The shuttling and paddling together was a factor, but ceremony also played a role. Each morning we smudged and were led, by Chuck, Shelley, or someone else, to be reminded of the sacred river we were paddling and to give thanks, *wanishi*, to the four winds and great spirits to guide us. That kind of gratitude creates a degree of mutuality and respect. Also, the reverberation of singers seemed to leave us in a trance.

I knew some of the concern behind their "by yourself" question: had you been by yourself when the stroke happened, likely no 911 and no helicopter.

Plenty of people like to spend time alone. I am one of them. Not that I don't enjoy people. Perhaps it has to do with the space I was afforded when younger, my own room and stuff. My sisters shared a bed when my grandmother moved in for a short time. Too, I was more likely to take advantage of the opportunity to disappear on my bike on a Saturday morning, usually to wander to one of the creeks on the river.

Solitude is of course different from loneliness, which is how we feel about being alone—solitude in a state of distress. Being separated from a group, or even at a party where you feel like no one understands you, can trigger fight or flight. In a way, it's adaptive, like stress eating, the body and brain responding to stimuli.

When Hoff was writing, about 5 percent of all households consisted of one person. In the United States today, more than one in four people lives alone. The pandemic seemed to exacerbate the stress of this situation. Of course, you can live alone without being lonely, and you can be lonely without living alone.

≈ ≈ ≈

I reached Pond Eddy at ten thirty. Hoff and company got there at ten. I liked trying to keep up with them. Maybe this was a way of curtailing loneliness.

And I saw yet more eagles soaring. Hoff seemed a lover of nature, but the only time he mentions birds is when he quotes poets like William Wordsworth. The word "eagle" comes up only when he mentions the name of islands.

They have made a remarkable comeback since the DDT era. In the 1960s, only four hundred pairs were known in the lower forty-eight. Now, thanks to conservation efforts and a ban of the pesticide, they are no longer endangered or threatened. The Pennsylvania Game Commission reports over three hundred nesting bald eagles in Pennsylvania in 2019. In New York, upward of five hundred pairs. The New Jersey Division of Fish and Wildlife reports more than 220 nesting pairs of eagles. Fewer than ten bald eagles were observed in the state in the eighties.

Even before DDT, eagles were hunted and seen as a nuisance to farmers. Testifying before Congress in 1930 (the year DDT was discovered), Gilbert Pearson, then president of the Audubon Society, noted that the eagle was near extinction in some places. H.R. 7994 would make it unlawful to hunt or capture the bald eagle (the golden was excluded), except when the birds were in the "act of destroying wild or tame lambs or fawns, or foxes on fox farms." Pearson testified that the birds never took lambs, although the golden did. That resolution was later signed by President Franklin Delano Roosevelt in 1940 as the Bald Eagle Protection Act, and it was expanded in 1962 to include golden eagles. Thanks in part to Rachel Carson (who noted their decline due to DDT), the bald eagle would become a symbol of the environmental movement when Robert Rauschenberg designed the first Earth Day poster in 1970.

But back in the 1890s, when Hoff cruised what is now one of the largest and most important inland habitats in the United States, he did not mention eagles. Why? I posed the question to Diane Rosencrance, director of the Delaware Highlands Conservancy, who sent it to her Eagle Watch volunteers, composed of members of the National Park Service and the US

Fish and Wildlife Service. Tom Wittig, eagle coordinator with the USFWS, thought hunting would have played a major role, but habitat destruction too: "if a significant proportion of the mature forests were cut down, there would have been a corresponding decrease in the number of viable nest trees."

Others wondered if water quality was a factor. Logging would have degraded water quality and hence the fishery. Plus, there were tanneries on the upper Delaware, industries that used the acidic tannins in hemlock bark to make leather. And there were quarries, mills, and slaughterhouses, and the erosion, slurry, and offal they created would have had an enormous impact on the watershed.

I learned from Kathy Dodge, of the Northeast Pennsylvania Audubon Society, that the Upper Delaware was the first Important Bird Area in the country. It's a distinction given to areas that supply critical habitats for breeding, wintering, or migrating birds. But to earn that designation, you need people to watch and count birds, and their club was aging. Like the Lenape, they wanted an influx of younger people. Kathy also had concerns that climate change on the coasts could bring more people and development. She felt the influx of Covid refugees was a preview. We "need to keep this a place people would want to come to."

If the eagles were there, Hoff paid them no heed, but they are remarkable to see, even if becoming more common—wingspans as long as my paddle. One day with the Rising Nation, someone thought they saw one in a tree. "Just a crow," I said, realizing how stupid it sounded as it came out. Just a crow, that can use traffic to crack nuts, that mates for life, with more brain to body ratio than humans (especially this human). Let me never cease to find joy and beauty in the ordinary and familiar as much as the exotic and new.

In *River Notes*, Lopez writes that he "lost" some sense of himself by the river. A hawk, not an eagle, views him at a bend in the river from above, like he was inseparable from the river bend, "like a salmon or a flower." That single perception "has dismantled my loneliness."

≈ ≈ ≈

Around midday, the river started to get more crowded with rafts. Four guys plunged right over a ledge, but the raft was forgiving. Voices carried over the water and I heard a guy telling a story about jumping from a cliff into the water, getting the wind knocked out of him. His girlfriend was laughing. Modelo and music. Another crew thought the raft had a leak and I pointed out that the valve cover was off. "Thank you, brother."

Rafts are certainly more social but there are clear advantages to a canoe in flatwater in terms of ease of effort. The noise coming from the rafts reminded me of a kind of laugh track they used on the TV I used to watch in black and white to signal to viewers what was mildly funny and what was supposed to be hilarious. But was the laughter out here infectious or further reminding me that I was out here by myself? The outsider, the Zane Grey cowboy.

An irony of loneliness is that we can feel it when surrounded by people, like in a big city. I felt it less last night, more today. From what I have read, we each have a different threshold of isolation—some of us need less social interaction. What I worried about before the trip, and some during, was that there was no one to reason with, to ask for advice. I would have to rely on my own judgment, yet we're often not as rational when we don't connect with other people. Think of those middle-of-the-night anxieties.

When my relationship with my wife came to an end but we still lived together, I entered what might have been the loneliest period of my life. With Covid restrictions kicking in, it felt a little like being snowbound with an estranged relative. We were shut in, mostly, riding out the virus. Social distancing and we were distant. Few words were exchanged, hardly a "good morning" or "good night." Loneliness is basically a longing for a connection, for interaction. We were preparing the 1890s farmhouse for sale, and I repainted some rooms. Going back over the clean lines by the window trim (some made of chestnut), I remembered some of the care that went into the first painting. It was our second renovation of a house, and I thought it would be the last. Loneliness might have come from a sense of futility, that the effort was for naught. Or it might have come from some lack of recognition (which would go two ways, I know). Recognize the effort of others, and they you, and you feel less lonely. And loneliness might have come from a lack of shared perception. When the vision of a home is no longer shared, you feel isolated. Bound up in all of it, I suspect, was grief.

≈ ≈ ≈

I paddled through Mongaup Falls, taking on a little water. Dave Simon told me a story about this rapid. At Mongaup, Dave could see a woman in distress, petrified. "You having trouble?" he asked.

"I want out," she said. "I'm so scared."

They were in the middle of the river, a moving current, so there was no easy exit. Instead, Dave asked for her paddle. He had her hold on to the side of his boat and escorted her through the rapid. At the bottom, she took back her paddle, and was on her way, assured that the rapids below were not as dangerous.

At a rapid just below, Butlers Falls, Dave spotted two young kids, eight to ten years old, in a raft. "Save my grandpa!" they were saying. "Save my grandpa!" Then he saw a head bob up and threw the man a rope. He gave a stern lecture on not wearing a life jacket. The man didn't appear to understand, so the man's son-in-law, also in the raft, translated. He translated the whole safety briefing. Even if you go in for an intentional swim (as opposed to the accidental kind) wear your PFD. At a restaurant in Milford, where Dave was later dining, the same family came in. The man thanked him, again. His wife, in tears, did as well.

The views there and below, with Hawk's Nest Peak, were spectacular, with sheer cliffs rising to the left. Hoff thought the surroundings could easily be likened to one of the Colorado River's famous canyons. He had likely never been on the Colorado, and while the present scenery could not equal the Grand Canyon, it was a gorgeous view.

Earlier that summer I floated the Middle Fork of the Salmon River in Idaho with a commercial guided trip. The scenery there was sweeping, breathtaking, surely rivaling the steep canyon to the south. I was with a friend who engages with everyone, has an easy laugh. Some of that isolation crept in, but also, both there and here, I felt that crucial sense of smallness. It's the feeling we get from encountering something vast and wondrous that challenges our comprehension. In an awed state, our jaw drops, the goosebumps form. Heart rate and blood pressure drop too. Beyond the physiological, there are prosocial effects to awe: less concern for self, increased generosity, and more cooperation. A river has a way of stripping away pride and pretense.

≈ ≈ ≈

Two kids stood on a rock ledge wanting to jump but trepidatious, knees knocking. "Think about the story you get to tell," the father said. Ah yes, that crucial connection to others, the story.

While cruising downriver, I kept an eye out for a former camping spot three friends and I had found some thirty years ago. A lot changes in a river year to year, but the curve of a river, the bones of it, stay mostly unmoved. This spot was near a small rapid, where a reef of rocks jutted out, and there would have been some railroad tracks above on the bank. The four of us worked together summers as housepainters. We called ourselves Intensity Painting Company, but we were hardly intense, unless it came to the lunches we ordered: whole pizzas, hoagies for all, on the company dime, "eating" into profits, and the rule was we had to finish everything. No slice left behind. We painted the houses of our parents' friends, or their friends, so we were never too rowdy. But paint spills, ladder misplacements, broken windows, did happen. As did a nearly constant ribbing from up on the ladders.

One weekend we drove all night to Narrowsburg with two aluminum canoes strapped to the roof. Late in the morning, we slept some in the family wagon, but then loaded the boats and headed downstream. And that night, around dusk, we added some magic mushrooms to peanut-buttered bread. I remember the rich green of the forest and the bioluminescent glow from a decomposing log, fox fire. Moss was velvety, welcoming. We ran through the woods, tried to balance while running on the rails, and found ourselves gripped by a compulsion to shed clothes and immerse in the water—at least I did. I remember crawling over slick rocks, sitting on one partially submerged, silver streaks of water rushing past and around me, and not being afraid. Normally, the lichen on a rock might gross me out, but I sat, marveled at the starry sky above, awed. Boundaries felt porous, fear absent, and underneath it all the pulse of the river and a kinship with prehistoric humans and bedrock before.

I don't know about my friends, but I experienced something like the dissolution of ego. (One of us was more skeptical. Staring at the glowing twig: "what is it? God? NOT!") In a 2006 study printed in *Psychopharmacology*, a team of researchers at Johns Hopkins gave thirty volunteers psilocybin, and they found it among the most meaningful experiences in their lives, comparable to the birth of a child. Two-thirds of the participants rated the experience, where they were also given eyeshades and headphones to facilitate an inward-focused journey, as among the top five "most spiritually significant experiences of their lives." One third said it was the most significant. A year later, the ratings slipped some, but participants reported improvements in their personal well-being, life satisfaction, and positive behavior change, all of which I think we the housepainters could verify.

In his bestselling book *How to Change Your Mind*, writer Michael Pollan examines the science of psychedelic drugs and their potential benefits. When the ego dissolves, he writes, so does "a bounded conception not only of our self but of our self-interest." What emerges is a self that is more "open-hearted and altruistic"—in other words, a self that is more spiritual—in which a new sense of connection or even love seems possible. However, Pollan concludes that an egoless realm of consciousness can also be attained through meditation, fasting, and near-death experiences, and aided by the tools of Eastern religion. The less we think about ourselves, the more connected we feel to what's around us.

Traveling down the length of the Mississippi River, Eddy L. Harris describes in *Mississippi Solo* his journey less as a vacation, which is external, and more as a process of knowing himself better and better. And "each day on the river I shed more and more of my external self." Harris, from St. Louis, had little to no canoeing experience, but as he gains in confidence, he comes to believe he is capable of almost anything. He also begins to understand what it means to be a Black American on the historic river. "I promised myself early on I would not make race an issue out here," he writes. He would live as he had lived his life on shore. But it became clear that "people will see I'm Black only moments after they see my canoe is green. Maybe even before." A friend reminds him that he was traveling from the north where people like him are scarce to the deep South "where feelings toward blacks are none too sweet." As his friend, Robert, says, "from where there ain't no black folks to where they don't like us much."

≈ ≈ ≈

A man named Mike floated in the middle in a tube. Normally I asked the questions, but Mike saw my loaded boat and asked me.

"How far you going?"

"Trenton."

His father did it with a friend in the thirties, in a canvas canoe like Hoff's. It was during the Depression and there wasn't much else to do.

Reaching his destination, he ditched the canoe in the weeds, took the train home, and went back a year later to retrieve it. It was still there.

Inland Port Jervis would seem an unlikely place for a port, but it was about halfway along the route of the old Delaware and Hudson Canal, which ran between Honesdale, Pennsylvania, and Roundout, New York. The chief canal engineer was John Jervis. In 1851 the Erie Railroad completed a line from Hoboken to Dunkirk, New York (near Lake Erie). "P. J." was about halfway on that line, too, a once important link between the East Coast and the American interior, a satellite of Manhattan.

With the closing of the canal and the decline of the railroad after the Depression, the city became less vital. It probably didn't help that Interstate 84 made it possible to bypass the town. When Hoff's crew arrived in 1892, they went to the shoe dealer's and the post office.

Stephen Crane lived in Port Jervis (Whilomville in his writings) from 1878 until 1883 and he visited the area frequently from 1891 to 1897. His 1898 novella, *The Monster*, is believed to be based on an 1892 lynching of a Black man, Robert Lewis, by a mob who accused him of assaulting a white woman. A grand jury indicted nine people for assault and rioting, rather than for lynching Lewis. *The Monster* is about a Black man horribly disfigured in a fire who becomes a social pariah. It's a study of prejudice and fear in a small town, confronting questions of race that were rarely examined this trenchantly by white writers in late nineteenth-century America. On the 130th anniversary of Lewis's murder, a plaque was dedicated at the site of the atrocity. Erected by the state of New York, it reads: "Racial Lynching. On June 2, 1892, Robert Lewis was beaten, stabbed and lynched by a racially motivated mob. A great injustice is recognized."

In 1885 the writer John Boyle O'Reilly arrived in Port Jervis with three companions to canoe down to Philadelphia. He published his 1886 account, "Down the Delaware River in a Canoe," in the *Boston Pilot*, an Irish-American newspaper that he would serve as editor. O'Reilly was born in Ireland in 1844, a year into the famine. He later joined the Irish Republican Brotherhood, later known as the Fenians, for which he was sentenced for treason and shipped into penal servitude in Australia. He escaped to Philadelphia in 1869 and then Boston, where he made a career as a journalist, writer, and poet. The same year he arrived in Port Jervis, he gave a speech in defense of the rights of Black citizens at Faneuil Hall before the Massachusetts Colored League: "So long as American citizens and their children are excluded from schools, theaters, hotels, or common conveyances, there ought not to be among those who love justice and liberty any question of race, creed, or color; every heart that beats for humanity beats with the oppressed." His biographer, James Jeffrey Roche, paid tribute to him for his defense of "the oppressed negroes, as he had defended the oppressed Indians, as sincerely and zealously as he had all his life defended the oppressed of his own race. It was morally impossible for him to do otherwise."

≈ ≈ ≈

I found a spot to climb up the bank from the river and walked to the restored Erie Hotel, next to the old railroad depot, only blocks away from what was the Delaware House, where Robert Lewis was a coachman. At the bar I ordered a Fiddlehead IPA and a pastrami Reuben. The couple next to me each ordered Bloody Marys, and then two more. The bartender said she was keeping the mixture light because the weather was so hot. I was somewhat aware that I had come off the river and likely smelled like I had been paddling all day in the sweltering sun, but that cold beer and hot pastrami were good going down.

After that late lunch, and the bridge that carries Interstate 84, I stopped by Tri-State Rock, a small stone monument with an embedded bronze bench mark. New York, New Jersey, and Pennsylvania intersect here, and the monument is located in all three.

Below this the valley widened some, and there began to appear many more islands, some rising ten to fifteen feet above the river, heavily wooded.

At Quick Island I went left, and though only rated a I+, felt it one of trickier rapids yet. It followed around a bend, through a swirling whirlpool, the eddy lines wanting to grab our momentum, shift balance. The bow caught the upstream eddy, the stern and momentum still moving downstream, and the swirl between them nearly caused us to capsize.

Quick Island is named for Tom Quick, the "avenger of the Delaware." The Quaker William Penn generally brought peaceful ideals to his dealings with Natives. He thought settlers and the Lenape could live together, not that promises weren't broken. Two of Penn's sons convinced Natives that their father, who they respected, had a deed for all lands within a day-and-a-half walk from Bucks County. The Lenape presumed this to be about forty miles. In 1737 the Penn brothers sent runners, not walkers, to cover that territory, reaching seventy miles to modern-day Jim Thorpe on the Lehigh. The Walking Purchase, as it would be called, would strip away land the size of Rhode Island.

The city is named after Jim Thorpe, the Native American (Sac and Fox Nation) who is widely considered to be one of the greatest athletes in American history. Thorpe won gold in both the pentathlon and decathlon in the 1912 Stockholm games but only recently had his medals reinstated, more than a century after he won them. They were stripped for breaking strict amateurism rules. Thorpe's family and others believe the decision unjust and racist. In 1982, the International Olympic Committee declared him the joint winner but did not restore his records. Finally, 110 years later, it recognized him as the outright winner.

Instead of burial in his home state, Oklahoma, as his will requested, Thorpe's third wife, Patricia, auctioned his body to struggling coal and railroad towns in northeastern Pennsylvania that were willing to change their name to Jim Thorpe. One did, in hopes it would boost tourism. That town was Mauch Chunk, a name derived from the term *mawsch unk* (bear place) in the Munsee-Lenape language, a reference to Bear Mountain, which resembled a sleeping bear. Thorpe's body was spirited away the night before a burial ceremony on sacred lands. Legal challenges from Thorpe's family and the Sac and Fox Nation in Oklahoma to return him to his homeland have failed.

Thorpe did have a connection to Pennsylvania. He was sent to the Carlisle Indian Industrial School in Pennsylvania, which opened in 1879 with a mission to "kill the Indian, save the man." It was the flagship school of the US government's attempts to assimilate Indians and basically drain them of all their culture, language, dress. The school cut their hair, dressed them in military uniforms, forbid them to speak their native languages, and Christianized them. That kind of cultural genocide became the model for off-reservation Bureau of Indian Affairs boarding schools, not to mention the culture at large. Chuck Gentlemoon DeMund's grandfather was also taken from his family and enrolled in the Carlisle Indian School.

Quick's father, Tom Sr., built a cabin in the Milford area in 1733. He had been friendly with the Lenape and they with him. However, on a winter day in 1756, two years into the French and Indian War, Quick and his two sons crossed the Delaware to inspect some farmland. They were ambushed by Lenape who had aligned themselves with the French against the British, and the elder Quick was scalped. Tom Quick Jr. vowed to avenge his father's death. Even after the war ended, his campaign continued until his death in 1796. Tales of his killing a hundred Indians portray him as both cunning and merciless, but they blend fact with fiction. Some depict him as a hero but today he seems more a murderous psychopath, disconnected from the human community. Quick has been called a "loner who never married" in one newspaper account, which may remind one a little of present-day mass shooters. But the "loner" label may also be self-protective because if the shooter is a loner, he is not one of us. Violence doesn't always come from not belonging.

The town of Milford erected a monument in 1889 to "Tom Quick, the Indian Slayer." More than a hundred years later, in 1997, a vandal destroyed it. It was rebuilt and some people in town wanted to return it, wanted to memorialize a killer, and that brought protests, including from Native groups, and it remains in storage.

As Chief Chuck Gentlemoon tells it, his ancestors granted the Quick family the land, on the condition that their people could have access to the river for fishing and hunting. After a few years, Quick harassed them whenever they were in shooting range. The Lenape asked for a council, and he said to meet them in the barn, because he didn't want "stinking Indians" in the house. The barn ended up catching fire—either because the tribe lit it or he did. Quick tried to escape down the river, using a barn door as a raft. The Lenape caught him and killed him. Tom Jr. saw this and swore revenge. Chuck's father told him to "never get in trouble in Milford and never trust a Quick."

≈ ≈ ≈

Under the Milford bridge, I saw a lone black bear cruising up the hillside and off into the woods. I was coming up on Minisink Island and had to decide about going left or right. A barred owl called from the left, arguing for it, "who cooks for you?" I cook for myself, thank you very much. To the right, a raft of mergansers, arguing for that side. Maybe loneliness is a result of not liking the choices ahead of you, but the good thing about a river trip is that there are always choices to make, but not so many they become overwhelming, like the infinite amount of music or videos to "stream." I split the difference and aimed for the middle, parked just right of the point.

Hoff camped somewhere near Milford with "the influence of the sur-roundings" affecting him in many ways. While the others talked about botany and European travel and Shakespeare, the scribe went off into his "bad habit" of "thinking and smoking tobacco." He wrote in his journal that the "night's camp at Milford was remembered as one of the most pleasant of the trip."

Minisink Island is two miles long. *Minisink* means "at the island" from the Munsee-Algonquin *minis*, or island. The Munsee (or Minsi) were a northern sub-tribe of the Lenape. A sizable community of them were said to live here, but it seemed just me now. A pair of kayaks drifted past playing bluegrass on a speaker, which made me a little homesick for the mountains of Virginia. The paradox of river travel: leave home to feel more at home.

I had reception on my phone so I checked in with a few people, which might have assured them I was okay but increased loneliness just a smidge. Our devices connect us to friends and families but they can also leave us feeling farther apart. At the same time, you can feel more comfortable in your solitude when you know others care. When I checked my phone, I learned that the singer Nancy Griffith had died at the age of sixty-eight. Devastated, I clicked on a link to hear her and the late John Prine, who died in 2021 as a result of Covid, singing a duet, "Speed of the Sound of Loneliness," *out there running just to be on the run.*

I sat on my stool on a cobble bar at the tip of the island. Just behind me was some wood from a flood—logs heaped in a tangled crisscross. And behind that the island rose to taller and taller trees. If the self was an island, I was on the part that could be submerged when water rose. That part that could be let go. A British word for island, especially for one in a river, is a *holm*, pronounced like home.

I thought of some of the people I'd recently met, of those that helped me get here, those I'd shared the river with, this river, other rivers and trips. Those who once inhabited this island. The owl still called from the forest on the other side, closing the distance between us. In the otherwise quiet dark, it was a good holm for the night.

The Milford-Montague Toll Bridge, built in 1953.

DRIFT

Day 5—Milford (Minisink Island) to Tocks Island
245-217

Saturday morning, and the biting flies were bad. It was warm but I pulled on long pants, long sleeves, to cover my skin. The pesky insects still found the flesh between legging and sock by the ankles. Sully wanted back in the tent I was tearing down. She tried to find relief in the bushes and weeds, cover her hide from the menace. They looked like normal houseflies but seemed like some mutant strain: superflies.

I broke down camp and shoved off. At canoe-cruising speed they abated somewhat. But any buzz at all sent Sully below the canoe seat.

We were early and there was a fine fog on the water, a veil on the cliffs to river right. Gradually the fog dispersed, as flakes of sun beamed through the trees. Only a few puffs of smoky vapor hung on the water.

I wanted to get away from the flies, but I also wanted to slow down, enjoy the view. I was halfway by now or would be at some point in the day.

It was a Saturday morning in August when Thoreau began his "week" on the Concord and Merrimack Rivers, though really it was two weeks.

For his experiment at Walden Pond, which is where he went to write *A Week*, and get over the death of his brother, his paddle partner on the river trip, he compressed a two-year stay into one.

Quoting Jeremy Belknap, "the" historian of Massachusetts, Thoreau wrote, "In the neighborhood of fresh rivers and ponds, a whitish fog in the morning lying over the water is a sure indication of fair weather for that day; and when no fog is seen, rain is expected before night." If Belknap and Thoreau were right, it would be a fair day.

Although outwardly a travel narrative, *A Week* is also a book about an inward journey, into self, nature, the infinite. He structures it by his days and tucked into "Wednesday" is a transcendentalist poem, "The Inward Morning." The outer clothes "which outward nature wears," bring forth a ray of peace that "illumes my inmost mind."

In *Walden*, Thoreau refers to morning as a time our senses, creativity, and ability to reflect are the most heightened. He writes that "every morning was a cheerful invitation to make my life of equal simplicity, and I may say innocence, with Nature herself." Morning brought prospects of hope and renewal. He praises a "perpetual morning," too, a spiritual awakening. "Morning is when I am awake and there is a dawn in me," he claims, and wanted us to learn to "reawaken and keep ourselves awake, not by mechanical aids, but by an infinite expectation of the dawn, which does not forsake us in our soundest sleep."

I had made a coffee to go, but Thoreau suggests a more important way to stay awake. If we could only cultivate the emotions of (most) mornings and carry them through the day, we would be much better off. That taming of the head, so embroiled in detail and delusion (or biting flies), calls attention to the fact that nothing is permanent, we are always capable of changing things—yesterday need not define us.

A Week never sold as well as *Walden*, which fared a little better, but he retired to the pond in 1845 to write his river book, not what eventually became his pond book. The publisher printed 1,000 volumes but returned 706 of them. In his journal, Thoreau famously wrote that "I have now a library of nearly 900 volumes over 700 of which I wrote myself." Just a few years earlier his brother John, who he took the river trip with, died of lockjaw in Thoreau's arms. Just two weeks later, Emerson's son died of scarlet fever. Thoreau's journals, of nearly two million words, break off for six weeks after these losses. Thoreau was there in the woods to figure out what really mattered. If in *Walden* we can hear him bragging "as lust-ily as Chanticleer in the morning," we can also hear someone clawing his way back to daylight.

The Concord River was known as the Musketaquid to Pennacook Indians, which meant "meadow" or "grass-ground" river, for the way it flowed sluggishly through wild grasses and sedges. Thoreau named his boat the *Musketaquid*, bought for a week's labor. In 1842, Thoreau sold the boat to Nathaniel Hawthorne for seven dollars and a rowing lesson, glad to be rid of a reminder of his grief. Hawthorne thought "Mr. Thorow" (spelling as Concord pronounced it) "in want of money," living "a sort of Indian life" in Emerson's care. Then living at the Old Manse (Emerson's home), Hawthorne renamed the boat *Pond Lily*, but was disappointed he was not able to operate the craft as easily as Tho-reau, for whom it seemed "as docile as a trained steed," according to the Thoreau biographer, Laura Dassow Walls. Robert Thorson, author of *The Boatman: Henry David Thoreau's River Years*, has said that Thoreau liked to take his boat out and just sit and drift. "And drift, and drift, and drift."

From his attic room on Main Street in Concord, Thoreau wrote that "my window looks west," to the Sudbury River, about five hundred feet away. He had placed his bed so he could rise and see it first thing in the morning. On July 22, 1851, he wrote: "Before I rise from the couch, I see the ambrosial fog stretched over the river, draping the trees . . . as distinct as a pillow's edge." In his journal, Thoreau delighted in the way the river marked the change of seasons. Unfortunately, the river also marked the place of commerce, changed and managed by human intervention. But the river was a place where humans and nature were more entangled. The pond was a reprieve, a spot in time, but the river was the ebb and flow of life.

"I was born upon thy bank, river," he wrote in an unpublished poem, part of the original manuscript of *Week*. "My blood flows in thy stream."

And thou meanderest forever
At the bottom of my dream.

After writing about all the fish in the river, the shiners and suckers, perch and pickerel, horned pouts and sunfish, Thoreau arrives at the shad, "formerly abundant here, and taken in weirs by the Indians, who taught the method to white settlers"—"until the dam." That at Billerica, and the factories at Lowell, put an "end to their migrations hitherward." He feels rather bad for the shad, "Poor shad! where is thy redress?" He imagines them wandering the sea in "scaly armor to inquire humbly at the mouths of rivers if man perchance left free for thee to enter." They are full of instinct, "which is thy faith," now turned adrift, looking for where "men do *not* dwell, where there are *not* factories."

Thoreau writes that if those fish would be patient, after a few thousand years, "nature will have leveled the Billerica dam, and the Lowell factories, and the Grass-ground River run clear again, to be explored by new migratory shoals." But Thoreau had another thought: "Who knows what may avail a crow-bar against that Billerica dam?" At length, he continues, that it is of interest not only to the fishes, but the people of the surrounding communities, to "demand the leveling of that dam."

Thoreau's thoughts on dam leveling, crowbarring, link him to that more modern-day monkey-wrencher, Edward Abbey. In his "Down the River" chapter from *Desert Solitaire,* Abbey and his friend Ralph Newcomb set off in their rafts to explore a section of the free-flowing Colorado River, through Glen Canyon, Abbey's omphalos, soon to be the site of a "goddamn dam." The lake would supposedly honor but actually "dishonor, the memory, spirit, and vision of Major John Wesley Powell, the first American to make a systematic exploration of the Colorado."

Powell, who lost his arm in the battle of Shiloh, trained as a geologist and later became director of the US Geological Survey. In his explorations of the American West, and his study of geology and hydrology, Powell concluded that the climate was variable and cyclical, governed by the condition of aridity. Rain would not follow the plow, as the myth went, but pioneers would see their crops, and dreams, withered and spindly. He warned that overdevelopment would lead to devastation, unchecked optimism to ruin. But the desert Southwest continues to grow at a dizzying pace, twice the rate of the national average, and in the summer of 2021, after years of drought, what some are calling a mega-drought, Lake Powell was at 30 percent capacity. Water levels fell to the lowest point since 1969, more than 150 feet below "full pool" (the dam was built in 1963 and didn't reach full pool until 1980). Climate change is making it unlikely that lake levels will ever return to what they once were. As temperatures rise and evaporation increases, it takes more rain or snow to produce the usual amount of runoff.

Abbey and his companion drift downriver, "thinking river thoughts," a dreamlike voyage. "Down the river we drift in a kind of waking dream, gliding beneath the great curving cliffs with their tapestries of water stains, the golden alcoves, the hanging gardens, the seeps, the springs . . . the royal arches in high relief and the amphitheaters shaped like seashells." For Abbey, and others, the beauty they are passing through will be forever lost, buried under mud. Abbey hopes the dam builders will run out of cement, or slide rules, or perhaps "some unknown hero with a rucksack full of dynamite strapped to his back will descend into the bowels of the dam; there he will hide his high explosives where they'll do the most good, attach blasting caps to the lot and with angelic ingenuity link the caps to the official dam wiring system in such a way that when the time comes for the grand opening ceremony, when the President and the Secretary of the Interior and the governors of the Four-Corner states are all in full regalia assembled, the button which the President pushes will ignite the loveliest explosion ever seen by man, reducing the great dam to a heap of rubble in the path of the river." The resulting rapids he would name Floyd E. Dominy Falls, after the then chief of the Bureau of Reclamation.

Some twenty years later and miles upstream on the Green River, above the confluence with the Colorado, Abbey documented another river trip in "Down the River with Henry Thoreau." From Mineral Bottom to Spanish Bottom, the confluence with the Colorado, he stages a dialogue with "Henry." He does not think Henry would approve of his "gourmandising," his usual breakfast beer. "To hell with him. I do not approve of his fastidious puritanism." Nor does he approve of his celibacy. Though he grants that Thoreau was twice turned down by separate women, he finds Thoreau a "spinster-poet." Still, Abbey acknowledges that Thoreau becomes more necessary and significant with each passing decade. "The deeper our United States sinks into industrialism, urbanism, militarism," the "more poignant, strong, and appealing becomes Thoreau's demand for the right of every man, every woman, every child"—dog, tree, snail darter—"to live its own life in its own way at its own pace in its own home." Adding, "or in its own stretch of river." Wherever there is a living river, "Henry Thoreau will find his eternal home."

I floated that same section with my adult children three years ago. At breakfast, before we launched, there was some fighting between them that soured feelings. But sky and spires were high if the mood wasn't.

Eventually we found our way to the confluence, mouths agape in awe. And we climbed up out of Powell Canyon, retracing Powell's steps. I think I knew the exact crevices Powell writes of that would "admit the passage of our bodies," climbing "as men would out of a well." Despite squabbles, we had to work together on the climb: find the rock cairns, look for the good holds, hoist or hold each other, pass the supplies. The metaphors seemed as tangible as the handholds: keep climbing, help each other, watch for scorpions. Eventually, like a river, things come together. On top, we spied the braid of the ruddy Green on one side and the dun Colorado on the other—they are misnamed—the La Sal Mountains rose off in the distance. As Powell writes it (July 19, 1869), "And what a world of grandeur is spread before us! Below is the canyon through which the Colorado runs."

≈ ≈ ≈

The current and conditions were good that morning for river running. A little cloud cover meant it wasn't so hot. I hugged the shore so that when the sun rose overhead, the canopy provided some shade. I was conserving energy because I knew it would be a long day. There was an S-turn ahead, Walpack Bend, where the river makes a U-turn, heads north, and then another, back to the south. The curvy bends add about three miles to a straight-line distance. Sometimes, I have been warned, headwinds can be bad. Letcher warns that to attempt this whole section in a single day "requires considerable stamina of muscle and mind."

I almost made an excursion that morning to nearby Grey Towers, the estate of Gifford Pinchot, founder and first chief of the US Forest Service. Hoff found the "commodious lawns" of "Gray Castle" pleasing, under "fairy bowers of feathery spruce and pine." He was visiting the site of the man he called "Banker" Pinchot, Gifford's father James, who built the estate that is now a national historic site. "Forester" Pinchot would grow up in privilege, his father among the mercantile elite and his grandfather an owner of vast acres of timber. The "fairy bowers" were once stumps, yet because of the misuse of the forest that his family prospered from, mainly through his wallpaper business, James encouraged his son to study forestry at Yale. He would endow the Yale School of Forestry with $250,000, and the school used Grey Towers for fieldwork until 1926. James Pinchot hired architect Richard Morris Hunt (who designed the palatial Biltmore Estate in Asheville, North Carolina, where Gifford also worked) to design the forty-four-room, twenty-three-fireplace mansion with three sixty-foot turrets. It sits on a promontory overlooking the surroundings and river, towering above the landscape.

"Giffy" even had his own playhouse, the Bait Box, and Pinchot took some of that dominant view into his ideas about conservation, believing forests should be used wisely but used to benefit humans nevertheless. He managed America's forests by a simple utilitarian credo: "The greatest good, for the greatest number, for the longest time." It sounds strikingly like definitions for sustainability: meeting the needs of the present without compromising those of future generations. He was generally opposed to preservation simply for its own sake, putting him at odds with his mentor and Sierra Club founder, John Muir, who resisted the commercialization of nature. (The Sierra Club has distanced itself from its former president who, for all his veneration of "divine" nature, as Justin Nobel writes, regarded Indigenous people as "subhuman" and was unwilling to see past the prejudices of his times.)

In the early 1900s Muir led the Sierra Club in a losing fight against a dam in the Hetch Hetchy Valley, part of Yosemite National Park. According to Muir, damming Hetch Hetchy was a blasphemy. You might as well deface the world's great cathedrals, he wrote, "for no holier temple has ever been consecrated by the heart of man." Pinchot supported creating the reservoir to provide resources for San Francisco's growing population.

Pinchot brought a social justice philosophy to resource management, wanting to repair both land and human society. His wife, Cornelia, supported women's suffrage, endorsed birth control, and condemned sweat shops and child labor. She also made a significant financial contribution to the establishment of the NAACP. But Pinchot was a delegate to the first and second International Eugenics Congress, in 1912 and 1921, and a member of the advisory council of the American Eugenics Society from 1925 to 1935. Historian of conservation Jedidiah Purdy writes that we should "acknowledge just how many environmentalist priorities and patterns of thought came from an argument among white people, some of them bigots and racial engineers, about the character and future of a country that they were sure was theirs and expected to keep."

≈ ≈ ≈

I was joined on this stretch not by rafts but canoes, fleets of red ones. Canoes better fit this coming segment, as they are generally better for long, flat distances. But to novices, canoes can be tricky and tippy, and one group in front of me zigzagged like the river ahead, yet to figure out how to steer the boat straight. They chose a narrow channel through a small island. I heard scraping, and then what sounded like them running into tree branches. When I approached from upstream, I saw them trying to detach the boat, duck the tree.

Downstream from the island, I looked back up, and they were still figuring their way through the narrow stream and tangle of debris. I saw a woman on shore in a National Park Service uniform looking upstream with binoculars. It was Ranger Casey, patrolling by kayak, joined by a volunteer named Debbie. They helped stranded canoeists, made sure they had life jackets, and ensured that they didn't grill where they were not supposed to be grilling.

"Sometimes we just make them aware of the weather—a coming storm. Where are you headed?"

I told her and she said she was jealous. Not a wow, as in long journey, or where's that? But I'd like to do that myself.

"And that's all you have?"

She was used to seeing canoes with two or three coolers, gear piled on top. The reason canoeists like this section is because of good camping. And the reason there is good camping is because of the National Park Service. And the reason the NPS was here, in uniform, was because of a dam, or a proposed one.

In 1962 Congress authorized a dam at Tocks Island, six miles from the Delaware Water Gap. It would have contained a lake forty miles long, all the way to Port Jervis. Most of the land would be condemned or purchased from local landowners. By 1970 the National Environmental Policy Act required a comprehensive review of all federal projects and demanded more assessments and impact studies to be provided by the Army Corps of Engineers. That slowed down the process of the land acquisition and allowed for more public comment. Residents from Warren County, New Jersey, and Monroe County, Pennsylvania, opposed the dam. In 1975 the Delaware River Basin Commission, composed of the four basin-state governors and one federally appointed commissioner, voted to shelve the Tocks Island Dam project. President Carter (a canoeist) signed a law in 1978 adding the forty-mile river corridor to the Wild and Scenic Rivers System. The land already acquired by the federal government was handed over to the National Park Service, and Delaware Water Gap National

Recreation Area, originally intended as a narrow swath of land around a reservoir, became a seventy-thousand-acre park with forty miles of what is today a free-flowing Delaware River. The project was officially abandoned in the 1990s. Today the river runs free and the Delaware Water Gap National Recreation Area hosts over four million visitors every year.

≈ ≈ ≈

After I chatted with Ranger Casey, Sully and I had the river mostly to ourselves. We stopped to stretch our legs at Dingman's Ferry access, named for the Dutchman who operated the ferry beginning in 1735. In the 1830s, the Dingmans built the first of several bridges, all wiped out in floods, until the current one was constructed in 1875. This Dingman's Bridge is the last privately owned toll bridge on the Delaware and one of a handful remaining in the country. It survived major floods in 1903, 1955, 2004, 2005, and 2006. An early logbook shows tolls of forty cents for a horseless carriage, twenty-five cents for a two-horse wagon, ten cents for a horse and rider, five cents for a bicycle, and two cents for a walker. Under the terms of the original charter, no toll was charged for traveling to church or a funeral, a custom still in place. Today it will cost you one dollar each way to cross the bridge.

At the ramp I chatted with Sonia Szczesna, reading and waiting for her friends. Her hometown was my destination, Trenton, so we talked more. With partner Adam Nawrot she had just completed a documentary called *Godspeed Los Palacos*. The film tells the story of a group of Polish university students who set their sights on leaving behind the Iron Curtain to paddle whitewater in the early eighties. They skillfully navigate not only rapids but the Soviet system to journey to the Americas. With little to no whitewater skills, homemade kayaks, barely enough supplies, and hardly a clue, they descend the world's deepest canyon—Colca in Peru—yet run afoul of the Politburo when they leverage their newfound fame to support Solidarity and democracy.

Sonia was looking forward to something a little less adventurous. She later told me they had cake, watermelon, and multiple pineapples, "because canoe luxuries."

I recognized the book she was reading, *All We Can Save*, an anthology of feminine and feminist voices on the climate movement. Editors Ayana Elizabeth Johnson and Katharine Wilkinson were both frustrated with how often women's contributions to the climate movement were being overlooked. The book also highlights voices of a younger generation who, like Greta Thunberg, bring a moral urgency to the climate conversation. The persuasion is no longer an appeal to reason: the world is warming, we know why, and we know what we have to do. That approach increased some in pitch over the years, adding to it some very dramatic graphs and photographs. But the younger generation, including the Sunrise Movement and Extinction Rebellion, goes for a more moral and personal approach. You have betrayed us, spoiled our future and dreams. I am being harmed, and you have failed.

Life on the ground is also shifting, as temperature records are broken and storms are more severe. The impact is becoming clearer, accelerating not only the climate but the anger and frustration.

The editors write that initially the book's aim was to highlight women leading the climate effort, but the book also "became a balm and a guide for the immense emotional complexity of knowing and holding what has been done to the world," while not giving up. All we can save tilts toward all we can salvage, including ourselves. While it is too late to save everything—some species and lives have already been lost—"it is far too soon to give up on the rest."

≈ ≈ ≈

It was two women personally affected who led the resistance to the Tocks Island Dam. Both Nancy Shukaitis and Ruth Jones were among the six hundred already displaced by the early dam planning land acquisition. They and those landowners formed the Delaware Valley Conservation Association to sue the federal government on behalf of those being displaced. Their suit was dismissed, but they kept working to save the river.

With other environmental groups (Sierra Club, National Wildlife Federation, American Canoe Club, Trout Unlimited, and the Lenni Lenape League) they then formed the Save the Delaware Coalition, creating more and more pressure on Congress to kill the dam. Maya K. van Rossum, the current Delaware riverkeeper, told the *Morning Call* that Shukaitis "felt this deep, emotional attachment to the river, as if it was her friend, a part of her life that she had been engaged with always." And with that attachment, there is little option but to protect and defend.

Shukaitis did not evoke the typical image of resistance in the 1960s. When the government developed the Tocks proposal, Shukaitis was a housewife. Her dedication of time and effort sparked an activist's spirit, despite it not being a traditional role for married women with young families at that time.

≈ ≈ ≈

Just before the S-turn, I overheard some canoeists talking. Many more were on the river now, and they were looking to nab primo camping. Each site is marked with a number and a brown NPS tent sign, firepit provided.

I wondered about this rush to campsites, and Kathleen Sandt, public affairs specialist with the Park Service, said they are working on a camping fee and a reservation system, some site improvements, which would include better solutions for human waste, and the addition of new sites to replace those lost to flooding. New sites would be clustered so more easily maintained. They were piloting the reservation system with large groups. All of this is spelled out in their visitor use management plan, for the Water Gap and scenic river above it, released in 2020.

A couple named Ed and Becky talked with another tandem in a nearby canoe about the Little League World Series game last night. They were telling the other paddlers that the Toms River, New Jersey, team was in, and so was one from "Pennsy." They said this with some pride, as if there was a corner on the baseball talent nearby, or perhaps in anticipation of a rivalry. They were out for three days and loaded down, a cooler for each day. I must have looked a little worse for the wear, or they looked at my cooler and took pity on me. They offered me a frozen bottle of water, and when Sully poked her head out, here have another. Take one more. They say *water* in my native tongue, *wooder*.

On the nearby Appalachian Trail hikers talk of trail magic. Here, a bit of river magic. To be honest, the midday sun made me a bit hazy. They hardly seemed like "outdoor" people, just recreational canoeists out to enjoy the weekend. In Becky's words, "we are here to get away from the craziness of it all."

I thanked them but pressed on, trying to push ahead of the race for campsites. Luckily, the winds blew favorable on both sides of the S-turn. The river narrowed and the paddling went well.

I passed a swim beach on river left, Turtle Beach, and then one on river right just downstream, Smithfield. Laughter and screams of delight emitted from both, a full house. Music projected over the water. Shukaitis would say that a silver lining of the dam proposal and subsequent turnover to state and federal agencies was access and a free-flowing river (and laughter) for all.

I took the right side of Tocks and drifted the length of the island. A monarch butterfly joined me for a stretch, on its own journey. Then a glamorous blue damselfly, sequined. I pulled into the downstream end of the island, with a little grassy knoll above to pitch my tent. The water was clear and gently flowing over freshwater mussels, a good sign for water clarity. They are not present if the area is buried under stagnant water.

Before setting up camp, I walked the island some. Somewhere here and in nearby Worthington State Forest are rock core samples that Shukaitis and the Save the Delaware Coalition studied. They examined cylindrical borings removed from the ground and noticed how unstable the deeper parts looked. The dam would be built on unstable glacial material, and a collapse would mean disaster for densely populated areas downstream. Another reason why the decision not to build the dam was the right one.

In the history of environmentalism, the Glen Canyon Dam built on the Colorado River in 1963 looms as one of the greatest losses. The Sierra Club's David Brower called the defeat at Glen Canyon "the darkest day of my life." He said it would come to be America's most regretted environmental mistake. But here on the Delaware was a victory. Here was something to celebrate. And even though we live in an increasingly wounded world, we should remember the successes. At the very least, we should keep alive the spirit of resiliency and pliancy that allows us to weather the coming weather.

The night was clear and cool. After a supper of soup, I paddled back upstream, drifting down, like those other drifters, Huck and Jim. "It was kind of solemn, drifting down the big still river, laying on our backs looking up at the stars, and we didn't ever feel like talking loud, and it warn't often that we laughed, only a little kind of a low chuckle."

The river sustained and soothed those two. Floating down the longest undammed river east of the Mississippi, I was glad the dam builders were long gone. By that time of night, the beachgoers had packed up too, but the sounds of their happiness still rang over the rippling current.

The Delaware Water Gap Toll Bridge (Interstate 80), built in 1953.

RIFT

Day 6—Tocks Island to Martins Creek
217–192

Dawn brought a bright feeling. The river still flowed and I had come so far. The temperature had dropped a little, which was welcome. As the sun tipped over the horizon, I surveyed my remaining supplies, which were getting a little low. I made a peanut butter and jelly sandwich for lunch and breakfasted on oatmeal.

I had left Sully on shore when I paddled up and drifted down at dusk. She often put herself to bed before I did and usually found her way to a coveted spot on my camp pillow. She did the same at home. When I turned in, I shooed her off but felt a twinge of guilt at denying Sully her comfort. She found a spot on the mat at my feet, let out a sigh, and curled up. What I love about Sully, about dogs in general, is that despite being kicked off the pillow, in the morning all is forgotten and she is glad to see me. And if I woke at 4 a.m. with my own sigh, scribbled something in my notebook, she still kept a protective eye on me.

Though it seemed we were alone, I heard a car that morning across the river. After packing up the tent, I paddled over to see. Sully was glad for more time on land. She took off to the woods where there were rich, dank threads, in and out of leaf litter: mouse, vole, mink, thin stream of urine of some lost kin, pale gold. Squirrels in plain sight but lost above, rabbit droppings, black beads, a symphony of smell. Smell is her keenest sense. When she's on a scent, three, four, or five times I will call her before I can break the spell. These same scents and visions would come to her again in her sleep, paws twitching, small yelp, almost wild again in her dreams. The warrior she was meant to be.

We walked on the Old Mine Road, a mostly single-lane, pot-holed, and in places, gravel road. This old road is considered the oldest highway in America. It preexisted the timber rafts floating to Philadelphia, was in place even before the Declaration of Independence was read in the city of brotherly love. First a Paleo-Indian trail, then used by the Lenape, the road was further developed to haul copper from mines near the Delaware Water Gap to about one hundred miles north, Kingston on the Hudson River. The mines were worked by Dutch pioneers who brought their toil to their brethren in then New Amsterdam—now New York.

The Park Service used to host concerts up near a settlement called Watergate. Bach, Bernstein, or bluegrass. In his guide to the river, Gary Letcher writes, "don't miss!" But I had heard they were closed. For that matter, Ranger Casey had informed me that the visitor center at the Water Gap was closed as well. They had never reopened after the lockdown.

People lived here even after the government's land acquisition. The *New York Times* ran a story in 1971 on the squatters of Tocks and the Old Mine Road area. After the houses were bought by the government and subsequently vacated by owners, people moved into the "free" homes. Walter and Harold Van Campen, two brothers in their early fifties, refused to sell to the government. Their family had been on Old Mine Road for four centuries. "Last November they came and put us under condemnation," Walter told the *Times*. "We're just a remnant of the Dutch," said Walter. "But that doesn't mean anything. The Indian was here before then."

The Army Corps of Engineers had a problem. They bought many of the homes, but money was tight, in part because the nation had embarked on a war in Vietnam. To raise money, they ran "house for rent" ads in New York papers, including the countercultural alternative *Village Voice*. Throngs of "families" and communes took to Interstate 80, not long after Woodstock, to create self-sufficient farming co-ops. One was called Cloud Farm.

They called themselves river people, but to the corps and others they were squatters. The throng spilled over into the Pennsylvania side. According to Richard Albert in *Damming the Delaware*, they lived in "tent camps, Indian teepees, homemade structures, and a variety of innovative hippie homes including a geodesic dome built on a raft" in the river.

By 1970 the corps was having second thoughts about being landlords. Some residents reported being harassed, shot in the thigh by unknown assailants with high-powered air rifles. Eventually, federal marshals accompanied bulldozers, but Banko Omedelli and Uwe Dramm, two leaders of the river people, climbed up on the roofs of homes. The dozers backed down.

They battled in court until 1974 when a paramilitary force of marshals and state troopers moved in for an attack. The river people were awakened and taken from their homes with no chance to collect possessions. The bulldozers moved in again and leveled the homes. Farm animals had to be relocated. Long-time residents weren't crazy about the "hippies," but they didn't like the dam either. And the press, kept away from the eviction, turned on the corps, increasing opposition to the Tocks Island Dam.

≈ ≈ ≈

A sign on a tree said, "Se deben usara salvavida." Use your life preserver. When I had checked my phone that morning for news from friends or family, I read that mask mandates were back on at the university where I teach, but I could live with that. What was hard to understand is why medicine and public health had become politicized, when it simply seemed something we would all benefit from. Shouldn't masks, or vaccines, be like life jackets—a good lifesaving idea? Of course, drowning is not infectious, so there was that difference. In protecting yourself pandemic-wise, you are also protecting others.

I passed by Shawnee Point with the red-roofed, white Shawnee Inn standing there. People were out walking dogs, checking their phones. While other large vacation havens have closed doors, the Shawnee Inn has survived, perhaps because of the golf course. The course is said to be the crown jewel of the property, built in 1910, and twenty-four of twenty-seven holes are located on a one-mile island. I took the narrow channel on the Pennsylvania shore and traveled under the golf-cart bridge, a wood structure that looked flood vulnerable. A cable was loose.

Heavy rain from an October nor'easter flooded the course that year. Jonathan Kirkwood, executive director of the Shawnee Institute, told the *Pocono Record* it was their third golf bridge to go out in 2021.

I saw quite a few golf balls in the water. So far, I had not lost anything or tipped. But I realized I was tempting fate by even thinking that, knock on wooden paddle. I had Foul Rift ahead of me later in the day. I kept up a routine of paddle, paddle, apply sunblock, repeat. No serious sunburn, but my feet were constantly wet from getting in and out of the boat, so a blister had formed between my toes.

I passed under the I-80 bridge, San Francisco to New York, and rounded the bend to Kittatinny Beach and the visitor center for Delaware River National Recreation Area. On the beach, Ranger Jodie was picking up trash. She found a lot of Capri Sun straws, once an emptied-out whole purse, including a calculator. I helped her, picked up a KIND bar wrapper, which it seemed most unkind to have left. A beer can bothered her in the spiky river grass. I was already wet, so I stepped in to retrieve it. She once waded in boots and all to pick one out.

≈ ≈ ≈

The cleanup of the beach would make Ruth Jones, whose family's canoe livery was here, proud. She had been here only a few short days ago, once again leading a cleanup, which she has for thirty years. I reached her by phone later, and she told me the story of the beach and cleanups.

Ruth's parents took out a loan to buy a mile of riverfront in 1941. Ruth's mother, Edna, named it Kittatinny Beach, after the nearby mountains. Kittatinny means "endless mountains" in Lenni-Lenape, which Ruth says is appropriate, for when you are paddling the river (or running a business) there are "endless mountains ahead of you." Her father, a German immigrant, built the flagstone staircase still in use.

A retired businesswoman, Ruth, now eighty-eight, has a solid head for numbers. She used to paddle about four hundred miles a year. She tells me she upset a total of five times, "and I remember every one of them." She loved paddling the river, especially when it was clean. "At fifteen feet, you could see the rocks below. No heavy industry or farms."

The business used to put about two thousand people a year on the beach for trips. But as more and more people used it, she began to notice the trash. At first, she had the staff out for cleanups, but knew they would need more help. So Kittatinny Canoes sent out a call for volunteers. "We would feed them a hot breakfast and a barbecued supper. Let people stay in our campgrounds." They focused on about seventy miles of river, from Barryville to the Gap. Over the past thirty years, she estimates they carried about nine thousand tires from the river and over four hundred tons of trash. "If you clean the river, people have a tendency to keep it clean." She was still out leading the effort this past summer.

For their volunteerism, they were invited to the White House by George H. W. Bush, after winning first place twice in the Take Pride in America campaign. A proud moment, but Ruth once had a serious feud with the federal government. She and her husband Frank did not think the dam was necessary or viable, so they fought it. In her telling, "the corps hated that we were fighting them." So, they took their land first, either as retaliation or to make an example of them. She and her family were told to get off their land in July of 1968. Ruth says the government paid $240,000 for the land. An appraiser later valued it at over $4 million.

The growing family found a farmhouse they liked off Dumfield Creek with a hundred acres. But it needed to be renovated. She asked for a two-week extension to finish the renovations. Peter DeGelleke, then supervisor of the Delaware Water Gap National Recreation Area, denied it. "That pissed me off. I was so angry." The US marshal came with eviction papers. Her young daughter Julie was beside her. Ruth looked at her and saw tears streaming down her face. As Ruth says, "my German temper got the better of me." She rolled up the papers and put them back in the marshal's hand. "You tell Peter to shove these up his ass. Now you get the hell out of here." She paused. "That marshal—his eyes grew big. He turned around and walked out the screen door." The family finished the renovations, taking their two weeks.

They couldn't move the beach, so they moved the boats, cottages, and tavern. The original tavern is now the NPS visitor center. With Nancy Shukaitis, Ruth formed the Save the Delaware Conservation Association. She provided canoes and supported the 1974 canoe trip protest led by then governor Brendan Byrne, trailed by reporters and TV crews. The dam was voted down the following year.

On September 1, 1965, President Lyndon B. Johnson signed the bill authorizing the Tocks Island project. On that same day, her father passed. "He died thinking his business would flourish in that same spot." However, when she reflects, she says she's pleased the area is protected. It would have become too commercialized and unnatural. "I'm glad it's preserved for my children and grandchildren to paddle on."

Jones and her son David, who was operating the business, sold Kittatinny Canoes in February 2021. Nancy Shukaitis died a month later.

≈ ≈ ≈

Ranger Kevin descended the very steps Ruth's father built, tallying every thirty minutes the number of people on the beach. I was the only person in sight that morning. He told me I had come at a quiet point in the day. "Come back in an hour." We talked about the legacy of those women. "Ruth and Nancy Shukaitis are two of the most interesting people I've ever met." The Park Service employees I met seemed proud of the legacy they left, wanting to continue it.

The other story here was high on the hills. In addition to a dam, the Tocks Island project would generate power by storing water in a glacial pond high on Kittatinny Mountain. A consortium of power companies had purchased the land and planned to increase the size of the pond and use it as a storage reservoir. Water released from there would flow through turbines, generating power.

When Hackettstown's Casey Kays first saw Sunfish Pond in 1961, he said, "Oh God, thank you for this." Kays, a janitor, did not believe he or anyone needed a big yard because there was so much public land nearby. The Appalachian Trail skirts its shores. Kays called the pond a "cathedral in the wilderness, a place to meditate and to reflect on my past." He signed a 1976 statement to Congress on the de-authorization of the dam, "help save ALL of the 'whispering waters' of Sunfish Pond."

I have hiked the trail to the pond in late June when the highbush blueberries are in bloom. Reach out and pick them without bending over, barely breaking your stride.

When news of the plans for the pond became known, Kays and a fellow naturalist, Glenn Fisher, organized to oppose it. They formed the Lenni Lenape League, wrote letters to the editor, and on Mother's Day in 1966, led about a hundred people on a well-publicized pilgrimage to the pond.

A year later, more than a thousand joined, including sixty-eight-year-old Supreme Court justice William O. Douglas. Douglas penned an article for *Playboy* magazine, "The Public Be Dammed," which began with these words, "The Army Corps of Engineers is public enemy number one."

On July 1, 1969, New Jersey Power and Light sold the land back to the state and it became Worthington State Forest. Kays and Fisher, their grassroots activism, launched a nascent environmental movement in New Jersey. The teach-in that became Earth Day, April 22, 1970, took place several years after this activism.

People in the parking lot were gearing up for hikes. A few looked like thru-hikers with serious walking poles and footwear. If you approached from the south, it would be the first glacial pond you would encounter on the Appalachian Trail. During the last (Wisconsin) glaciation, fifteen thousand years ago, the sheets stopped about here, just south of the Water Gap. At the time, the ice wall was nearly half a mile high, higher than the ridge is today (about 1,500 feet).

≈ ≈ ≈

Looking up, the sense of deep time made me woozy. Stories and futures written in the rock.

It's hard to imagine those events from long ago, but artists came here to paint images of the Water Gap. Famously, George Inness did in 1861. Hung in the Metropolitan Museum of Art, his *Delaware Water Gap* depicts a dramatic sky. A train emerges on the side and three people park on a logging raft in the middle of the river, tending a fire. Cows drink at the river's edge. Painted from the Pennsylvania side, a rainbow arches above the Gap, the mystical power of nature and a theme of the Hudson River School, only here on the Delaware.

It's an idyllic vision, but the Met provides this context from artist and cultural leader Joe Baker, a member of the Delaware Tribe of Indians in Oklahoma and director and cofounder of the Lenape Center in Manhattan: "Inness does little to portray the truth of an American genocide. The Delaware Water Gap . . . was the epicenter of colonial mayhem and capitalistic exploitation. By the time this pastoral rendering of peaceful commerce in the rural countryside was completed, my people, the Lenape, had been forcibly removed west to Indian Territory (Oklahoma), Wisconsin, and Canada. The environmental degradation caused by the Industrial

Revolution was in full swing seventy miles north along the Hudson River, forever changing the landscape of Lenapehoking."

The Sierra Clubs of Pennsylvania and New Jersey, along with former area superintendent John Donahue, have proposed changing the Delaware Water Gap National Recreation Area to the Delaware Water Gap National Park and Lenape Preserve. In the words of Donahue, the purpose of the redesignation would be "to place this gem of our national heritage into the jeweled crown of the national park system where it has always belonged." It would protect the resources, such as the river and the Appalachian Trail, and honor "the First People who occupied the area for millennia" with a Lenape cultural and education center.

The proposal is controversial because it is unclear if hunting and fishing would be allowed, though that is one reason for the "preserve." Hunting would be allowed in the outlying 56,000-acre preserve that would ring the 9,700-acre park. The Sierra Club contacted the Lenape, but those in Oklahoma, the Delaware, who gave their approval. But they did not contact the local nations. Chuck DeMund said he was not necessarily against the idea, but it would have been nice to have been asked. Said Adam Depaul about another renaming of a park downriver in Frenchtown, New Jersey, from Sunbeam to Sunbeam Lenape Park, "every instance of learning our name moves us forward."

Part of the purpose of their river journey was seeking recognition, including state recognition. As of yet, the Lenape Nation of Pennsylvania (LNPA) is not recognized by the state of Pennsylvania. There are state-recognized Lenape in New Jersey and Delaware, but none in the state of William Penn. Three federally recognized tribes exist, two in Oklahoma, the Delaware Nation in Anadarko and the Delaware Tribe of Indians in Bartlesville, and one in Wisconsin, the Stockbridge-Munsee Community. There are also several in Ontario. But the federal tribes do not support the state tribes gaining a foothold into recognition.

The standards for federal acknowledgment are strict. Groups must be able to prove their continued existence as tribal entities since at least 1900. Some two hundred years passed between the departure of the main body of the Lenape people to the west in the late eighteenth century and the founding of the LNPA in 1998. Even those that can offer proof face the steep financial cost of legal fees and documentation efforts. When they don't fit the criteria or lack the resources to engage in a lengthy battle for federal recognition, tribes generally work to become recognized by a state instead.

The Delaware Tribe of Indians claims that no Lenape people exist outside its membership and that of the other federally recognized nations. In 2015, their tribal council passed a resolution opposing "fabricated Delaware 'tribes,' 'groups,' and 'Indians.'" At the heart of this dispute is the fact that there are limited resources the Bureau of Indian Affairs can apportion to Native communities, and so tribes can be fiercely protective of their status. Tribal gatekeeping is one of the few mechanisms of control left for existing tribes.

The cruel irony is not lost on the LNPA. The US government, who removed Indigenous people from their lands, retains the power to confer authenticity on the very people who lived there first. At one of the treaty signings, I heard Sarah Bursky, a staff liaison for the National Park Service, "apologize for the pain" her government and employer had caused. In disputes about recognition, the recognized tribes take on the mentality of the colonizer, of settler logic.

Adam DePaul described it as a kind of Stockholm syndrome—affection by the victim for the captor. Adam had foregone the sunblock our first few days of the trip. Several days in, his sunburnt skin, including on his bald scalp, had bronzed. With two hands on his paddle, he often spoke over a cigarette draped from his mouth. He said they had reached out to the federal tribes but have not received a warm welcome. He set down his paddle and took out his cigarette, squinted. "It hurts us. It hurts all of us." DePaul thought it a problem of the recognition system itself, which divides people. He used a broken dish analogy for Samantha Spengler of *Philadelphia Magazine*: just because the dish breaks and you glue it back together, "you can't say it's never been a dish. You can try to say it's not a dish anymore, but if you do that, you have to admit you're the catalyst for that."

≈ ≈ ≈

The landscape would change greatly from here on down. To my left I had Mount Tammany, bold and rocky, named after the Lenape chief Tamanend. To my right, Mount Minsi, named after the Indigenous people of the area. The spires formed the gate through which I passed. Hoff called them "lofty, silent sentinel peaks." John McPhee writes that the big river cuts through here like a "thief through a gap in the fence." The peaks center and arrest the view like a "notch in a gunsight." These geological formations would give way to some rich soils, and below here the river and landscape would spread out. The river would shallow some too, with many islands. As Hoff described it, "one rift after another until sun-down."

At Portland, I pulled over under the pedestrian bridge and walked up the hill. The Portland Hook and Ladder Co. #1 was selling hot dogs for a fundraiser, so I placed an order for one. The woman handed me two, one for Sully. She stared at hers with reverence and took it gingerly as a gift too good to be true. Then she turned away from me as if hiding her treasure, or concealing her delight, and consumed it whole.

The hot dog was warm and tasty, the mustard tangy, but my supplies had dwindled, and I was really craving fruit. Maybe it was the thought of those blues up on the hill. Even more than a tube of meat, I would kill for an apple.

I had marked a farm stand in Ramsayburg on the car trip north. And it was coming up. I passed by docks, people out in boats, the dreaded Jet Skis. But I overshot the fruit stand. The mileage was off in Letcher's *Canoeing the Delaware*, which had it at 203.8, but I could hardly blame him (I was using the outdated book after all). I wound up at the Ramsayburg Homestead, which had a plaque to highlight the importance of commercial traffic on the river long ago, and one on some of the Durham boats made in the area, but *yada yada*, as we say in New Jersey. I wanted fruit.

I turned around and paddled upstream, determined. I found a place that looked good to tie up the boat, the bank not too steep. Then I walked through a place that appeared to be making mulch, and then by something like a garden with desiccating peppers. The stand advertised "fresh" produce, but the fresh appeared relative. The apples were from Chile, and the blues looked fresh only in that they had been refrigerated. Not from Jersey, where the blueberry was born. Elizabeth Coleman White, a native of Whitesbog in the Pine Barrens, is credited with developing the first cultivated highbush blueberry plant with the help of USDA botanist Frederick Coville. The berries thrive in the sandy and acidic soils of the Garden State.

Most disappointing, there were no fresh-looking or heirloom Jersey tomatoes. I asked where the corn came from and the clerk told me "just up the road," but who knows how far. Still, I bought some, and a Chilean apple. At the counter, the woman was making peanut butter and scooping it into containers. It seemed this, like the garden, gave the appearance of being "homemade," fresh.

I was starting to feel a little fresh myself. Back out on the river, I bit into my apple, but the Jet Skis swirled, so I had to keep both hands on the paddle, steady the boat. One guy was trying to make a whirlpool, just traveling in circles.

Another guy in a motorboat had music on over a speaker. Sporting a pot belly and a white muscle tee, he was talking on his phone while pulling his son on a wakeboard. The kid said he was tired. "Wha?" the father said. The boy repeated. "Do the thing," said the dad, making a circular motion with his hand. My daughter, a fan of the *Sopranos*, would say that is "so Jersey."

I passed a group on a pontoon boat. "How far you going?"

"Trenton."

"Awesome."

Is it? But then I saw an eagle rise from a tree. That is also Jersey. I had also seen the swirled ice cream sign for King Cole's roadside stand on the way up but it was closed. No big loss. I already had a hot dog, and now a song in my head: *Suckin' on a chili dog* . . .

Islands ahead of me. I think Wally (Hoff) stayed on the Jersey side. Gary (Letcher) didn't say which way the channel was (we were on a first-name basis now). At the tip of one island, people were out in chairs half in the water, kebabs on the grill.

"How are ya?"

So Jersey.

I passed by a town I had been to earlier in the summer. My son was hunting for a used truck and we found one here at a used car lot while we were visiting my family in Titusville. We liked the truck and a mechanic had approved it. I negotiated a price over the phone, but when we showed up to take delivery, the salesman wanted to charge a fee for using a check card. The warranty was also void because we were not paying the full price—"says right here in the fine print." The fee had put the price back up near full. Buying cars is stressful enough but even harder when you feel you're going in circles. And it would be hard to say why the mechanic's Jersey accent sounded blue collar and trustworthy to my ear but the salesman's, "those mechanics, they find every little thing," sounded like a con man, but I was as angry at him as I have ever been at anyone.

I paddled through several more rifts, Long and Buttermilk and Little Foul. Little Foul helped me anticipate big Foul, but big Foul already had a reputation that preceded it. It drops twenty-two feet in a half mile. Gary called it one of the most severe rapids on the river. People kept asking Wally what they would do about Foul Rift. "Each had some particularly horrible phase of Foul Rift to pound into our ears." In town they "heard nothing but Foul Rift, and how dangerous and swift it was." The naturalist John Burroughs, who lived in the upper watershed, wrote in a "A Summer Voyage" about his trip down the East (or what he called the Pepacton) Branch that passage through Foul Rift is accomplished with "no little danger." John Boyle O'Reilly, who canoed the river in 1885, heard it was the "foulest rapid on the Delaware."

What makes it foul? Jagged angular limestone rock, black and menacing, lava-like. The rocks are pockmarked, as if "pitted with a hideous smallpox" per O'Reilly. He described "teeth that lay in wait to lacerate the boats under the water-line." The timber rafts contended with those teeth and the drops, but paddlers today also spot smokestacks, power company cooling towers, making the scene even more ominous. I was again running a rapid late in the day. I stood to do a visual scan and chose the right line. I remembered reading, in Wally or Gary, that the Pennsylvania line was the best, so I veered that way.

I aimed for a seam where two separate flows braided together. I tried to miss the big wave so as not to take on too much water early in the rift. Take on water and the boat sloshes, becomes more tippy. The stern scraped on a submerged rock. Wally punctured somewhere here, a point cutting through his canoe like an axe. Boyle O'Reilly did too, one of the sharp edges slicing his boat "as a bravo does his victim."

My plan was to stay right, but there was "wood" at the bottom, a downed tree. Such obstructions are also called sweepers, for the way they can brush you out of the boat, or strainers when under water—a paddler can be trapped in the sieve. I started moving left toward the center, which looked ledgy and dodgy. At a certain point in reading a river, you're locked into the choice you made, and there's little to do but prepare for the impact, so I paddled forward hard, to at least bring some forward momentum into what was oncoming. In a kayak, such a stroke can launch one over a ledge. Not likely in a loaded boat, but we can try. We hit, rocked a little on impact, took on some water from a wave. But just after, still upright, no puncture, I yelled, an adrenaline release, a hell yes we made it. Sully joined me in the back, either to check on my sanity or join me in the celebration.

Wally hadn't noticed the cut on the way down, as his canoe was not "deflected from her course." But at the bottom, "I took the last drop at 11:20 with a great deal of water shipped."

He records the time, but he hardly notices the cut. I think that has something to do with the fact that in the rush of the rapid, the sound, speed, and force of the water, we are fully in the present, outside of time. I was. And at the bottom, a kind of ecstasy, which is like a merging of rivers or of identity—self, rock, river. In a rift you are thrillingly in now.

The trick, as many Eastern teachers tell us, is to bear such a present awareness into even unextraordinary times. Peter Matthiessen writes in *The Snow Leopard* of his goal "to be of the present, nothing-but-the-present, to bear this mindfulness of *now* into each event of ordinary life."

After repairing his boat, Hoff reflected more on Foul Rift. For amateur canoeists, he says, it is dangerous and had "better be avoided," as had Wells (Lambertville) Falls. But for canoeists "fresh from the trying school below Hancock, it should have no terrors." When the river is at a good level, it might even be done easily. "In fact, the people exaggerate its dangers from hearsay." Even after slicing through his boat, Hoff seems to be suggesting things are rarely as bad as we make them out to be. Perception overshadows reality. What's foul is fair.

≈ ≈ ≈

On the Lenape trip I met another professor, Storm Heter, who taught philosophy at East Stroudsburg University, near the Delaware Water Gap. He was born in Kansas on a night when a thunderhead rolled in on the Great Plains, and his hippy parents named him after the weather event. Thunderstorm was shortened to Storm.

His graying, shoulder-length hair belied a youthful spirit. Climbing and skateboarding were two of his favored pursuits, but he was taking to paddling. He had packed even more minimally than I had, stuffing eight days of food and gear in the hatch of his borrowed kayak. When I said I taught

English, he mentioned an essay by the late David Foster Wallace. Storm's mentor was his father, James Donald Wallace.

In his landmark commencement address at Kenyon College in 2005, David Foster Wallace began his case for a consciously lived life with a parable of two young fish swimming. They happen to meet an older fish heading the other way, who nods and says, "Morning, boys, how's the water?" The two young fish swim on for a bit, and then eventually one of them looks at the other and goes, "What the hell is water?" The point is that the most obvious, important realities are often the ones hardest to see.

Foster Wallace describes an ordinary trip to the grocery store and being annoyed at the line and the checkout lady who says, "have a nice day." For him, "petty, frustrating crap like this is exactly where the work of choosing comes in. Because the traffic jams and crowded aisles and long checkout lines give me time to think, and if I don't make a conscious decision about how to think and what to pay attention to, I'm gonna be pissed and miserable every time." If he doesn't choose how to think, his default setting is to think situations like this are really all "about me." It's basically an appeal to empathy, which Storm seemed to possess in abundance.

Heter wrote a book on existentialist philosophy and was an expert on the philosophy of Jean-Paul Sartre. From what I could gather while paddling near, existentialist philosophy says that we choose a meaning rather than have one chosen for us, at least if we would live "authentically." Existentialism is sometimes seen as championing the individual and disparaging community, but for Heter, it is deeply social. The notion of "authenticity," important to Sartre, requires both interpersonal recognition and group participation. We cannot be "authentic" in a vacuum, for the dynamic requires that others recognize us.

He spent a day by himself pre-trip, and then a week with the Lenape. He later told me by email: "On my own, I think I communicated with Lenape Sipu as an 'I.' During the trip, I felt that 'We' were communicating with the river. That feeling of 'We' was so powerful that it healed some wounds I've had for years, since childhood."

Part of that healing was learning about the how the Lenape Nation was healing. In addition to being a philosopher, he was a strong advocate for social and environmental justice. He disliked seeing the historical markers that touted some aspect of colonial history long forgotten. Instead, he proposed a new one with the title, "Stolen Land." It would say something

about how so-called Pennsylvania was home to Lenape and other Indigenous people before they were pushed off by European settlers who wanted
access to hunting, fishing, foresting, and other resources.

With boat docks and pontoon boats, the section just after, Hutchinson,
reminded me a little of my home stretch in Titusville. Only someone hung
a political flag or two that could knock me out of my present exhilara-
tion. My sense of optimism that the human forces of goodness, kindness,
community, and justice were slowly winning against forces of meanness,
narcissism, and racism had deteriorated in the past year. But I have tried,
still try, to focus on the work of people who continue to struggle to be a
force for good, not foul.

On the bank I spotted a tube labeled "WOW," like in the comics, called
"The Thriller." Lot of thrills out here.

At the very last dock, a man on a pontoon boat asked me, "how far?"

"Trenton," I said, more confidently now. I'll get there.

He gave me a camping tip on the downstream end of the coming island,
Kiefer, but when I arrived, a kayak had already claimed it. Damn. I pulled
around to the other side, dragged the boat up a narrow spit and found
a really good place to park and camp. There was a sandy section with a
long gravel bar. Someone across the river on the Pennsylvania side fired
shots for target practice, which put me back in the mind of heavily armed
militias. But the ammo will run out, and the noise won't last.

I parked my stool on the gravel bar and shucked and cooked my corn.
Swallows curled for insects in energetic, acrobatic sallies, contrasting with
my own fatigue. In the riffle to my left lay the upside-down frame of a
truck or trailer, rear tires still attached, half submerged. But the sunset
looked like it would be gorgeous, and was, viewing it out over the fork
spearing my ear of corn, beside the rusty axle. I rotated my corn in a really
good present. That too is so Jersey, this turn of the river.

Martins Creek Branch rail bridge, built in 1885.

CHANNEL

Day 7—Martins Creek to Frenchtown
192–162

The bird of the morning was a kingfisher, careening and rattling up the river. I was interested in meeting my Friday, but Sully snuck off and barked at him or her, so I kept packing. She barked out of surprise, or as a warning shot, a kind of test, but soon her tail would lower and foe would be friend.

I had very little life left in my phone, but had seen that a tropical depression was approaching, so I thought I should get in some miles, check updates later. I was glad to have the report, but a week in, I liked the device best in my dry bag. I passed the Riverside Bar with white tents on the lawn. Had I gone a little farther, I might have joined in the festive atmosphere.

Gray-hulled clouds sailed in. I was a little behind Hoff by now. He found lodging just below Easton in Raubsville. They had forty-four miles to Trenton, which they debated doing in one day. I had fifty miles in front of me, at least two more days until Titusville, another to Trenton. But the leaden sky was looking ominous, and I wasn't looking forward to camping in the rain. The gloomy atmosphere was heightened by a set of smokestacks from the Martins Creek cement plant.

I took a kind of inventory. So far, the only injury I had sustained was a sore under my ankle from where my sandal buckle rubbed. And my feet, because nearly constantly wet, had blistered. My pinky toe was raw. My hands had started to develop some blisters too. I put lip balm on the callouses. Sunblock doubled as moisturizer. In my arms and shoulders some soreness, but it also felt good to feel the strain in the ribcage, an opening in the thoracic cavity, with each paddle a breath. When you link your paddle to your breath, you feel connected to the river. Paddling becomes more a meditation than a chore.

I had to be careful of nicks and cuts. My doctors recommended a daily dose of aspirin to ward off the kind of clot that nearly killed me. Natives used to gather salicin (an ingredient in aspirin) from the inner bark of willows, which thrive in wet marshes and riverbanks, to reduce fever and inflammation. A bad scrape and my blood would spill into the river. Maybe it already had.

The river is lifeblood.

Nearly fifty miles to go? Keep the blood pumping. Less to home, where I could sleep in a bed and take a shower. Not that I was minding my river baths. I had taken a push-up version in the morning. The water was shallow so go in, plank position, lower, soap up, repeat. Immersion. On mornings like this, it was easy to see how, for the Lenape, everything has a spirit. But it has a body too, one we join with.

The key when tired, for the final push, is to conserve energy. All along, I have been trying to find the channel, the place where the flow is greatest, resistance the least. Line up for the channel and the river takes you. Where two channels come together, line up for the middle and slice through clean. And when the river bellies around a bend, smooth out the curve.

In the village below, it seemed they had put all that cement to use in walls, ramps, platforms. I could tell the water was a little low by the relative height of the non-floating structures. In these river towns, there seemed to be a community concept in boat and dock style, copying whatever worked.

Below there, what might have been a swim beach was in a sad state. A rusted ladder clung to a platform. Beer cans and trash. Letcher wrote that the city of Easton "hopes to develop a public beach and picnic area here." Those plans did not appear to have come to fruition.

I passed under Easton-Phillipsburg Toll Bridge. Easton is the largest city on the river except for Trenton (and Philadelphia). Suddenly, there are tall buildings. On the New Jersey side, Phillipsburg, some industrial word-art high on the street: *Collision. Salon Fashion. Jimmy's Doggie Stand.*

High up on the hill was Lafayette College, where my grandfather went, where my parents wanted me to go—but I longed to see the West.

I heard a rustle in some shrubs on the bank and a man emerged carrying a trash bag, plunged back in. He is Jake Aaron Book, black jeans, sleeveless black tee, holding two black bags, both full. He cleans both sides of the river weekly, removing trash.

Jake told me he both cleans and tries to stay clean himself, drug free. I told him, clumsily, that I mistook him for a homeless person.

"I am homeless," he said. "But I have been clean for ten years. I work construction five to six days a week. And I lead a team of volunteers." He calls his group, simply, Let's Clean. For Jake, cleaning the river was a kind of purpose. I poked around on shore and tossed a couple of cans in his bag.

For me, floating the river had been a purpose. And at a certain point in a river trip, the rest of the world begins to feel irrelevant. You find your routine. Let the water carry you. Although here in the city, I felt temporarily pulled back into the world. Up on top, there was a city alright. A few people walked around, and a guy in dreadlocks left his girlfriend on a park bench to free a goose from some fishing line, but it may not have been stuck and was rather just sticking to that particular piece of real estate. It hissed, so the man returned to his bench and observed.

I was just upstream from the confluence with the Lehigh River, the Forks of the Delaware, a commercial and strategic prize for centuries and the main objective of the infamous Walking Purchase of 1737. This is where the runners, not walkers, sent by the Penn brothers, ended up. The Lehigh flowed over a spillway, impounding water for the Delaware Canal. A plaque commemorated the Treaty of Easton, 1758, which tried to resolve conflicts created by the Walking Purchase. It specified that the Native American nations—including Iroquois, Lenape, and Shawnee—would not fight on the side of the French against the British. In exchange, Pennsylvania returned large blocks of land that the Iroquois had ceded a few years before, and the British colonial governors promised to recognize hunting grounds in the Ohio River Valley and to refrain from settlements west of the Alleghenies. We know how that went.

I thought it might be a kick to walk (not run) around some. A river rat with blisters in the city. Pizza anyone? That was one expectation I had before the trip. That there would be more time in the towns and taverns. But before long, I just wanted to get back in the boat. Back in motion.

In *Dopamine Nation*, Stanford psychiatrist Anna Lembke explains that dopamine is integral to our craving for movement. Dopamine is a neurotransmitter, part of the brain's reward system. When we lived in a world of scarcity, we needed a reward to seek our food, clothing, and shelter. A brisk walk still now releases it. A walk with a friend even more. Evolutionarily, we are finding food (or love). Yet at present we live in a world of abundance, barely needing to leave the couch to fulfill our basic needs. We find the high in other ways such as with screens or drugs, which can become addictive, until we need more and more of them to get the same high. By walking along the river filling his trash bags, Jake was possibly substituting one craving for another, but it was certainly a healthier form of addiction.

I have exercised regularly most of my life: run, bike, swim. When asked why? These activities, when I can do them, make me feel glad. The joys are simple but encompassing. Life quiets down to simple rhythms. Problems evaporate. Quite possibly, however, my stroke was caused by overdoing it—I will never know. When I broke down in a hospital, my thoughts ran to what if I could never paddle, or swim, or ride my bike, or hike a mountain, ever again? What if it happens again? What if I don't survive? Nerve endings might have been frayed, brain cells deprived of oxygen, but it felt like the only way back to recovery was to keep moving. Exercising might have killed me, but it might also have saved me, as the blood moved efficiently up around the clot to reach the right side of the brain from the left. I had to keep that blood flowing. Repair the circuitry though use, so I reasoned.

One subtle side effect of the stroke, one no doctor mentioned, is that it felt like my range of enjoyment had been reduced, the joy curve flattened. Very often, I carried around a dull fatigue, a bad case of the doldrums, stuck in cement. One way I felt like I could restore fullness was by getting up and walking. I was trying to gain back some momentum snuffed out, the vital energy and spirit it felt like I had lost. Even during the pandemic, when lockdown ensued, I had to move. I hiked Fourteeners in Colorado, rode my bike to Mountain Lake at my home in Virginia, paddleboarded on the New River. I sometimes experienced swells of anxiety. Is that a tightness in my neck? Who would I call if it happens? How would they transport me to the hospital? I have somehow learned to turn down the volume in this part of my brain, which is a good strategy overall—focus on what you want to happen, not what you don't. Also, riding downhill in an aerodynamic tuck, the view from a summit, balancing a board on a small wave while facing upstream, small irrepressible moments of laughter and delight.

Perhaps it was the disappearance of the sun, that disinfector and mood enhancer. Or maybe the trash made me think of patterns of mind I would discard if I could. During the pandemic, the world entered a collective depression, but add a stroke and separation, and I was down. I was treading water but sinking. I had dipped into those psychic troughs before, and it felt like sediment clouding the water, choking off the light. My way out was usually through movement. Tranquil walks in the woods return me to my senses. Or some startling discovery does. Shoo a moss-draped snapping turtle across the road, hissing as you help. Catch the buff belly and dark red tail of a hawk, nabbing something in the flaxen meadow, kneading the integument of its catch. Their wildness, satisfying a hunger, reminds you to pay attention, be alive. Out here, paddle and breathe did the trick. Even in such calm, I worried about how my brooding flowed downstream to my children, who have struggled with their own periods of sadness and melancholy.

A decline in mental health was underway before the pandemic, but it now seems a full-blown crisis, affecting young people across economic, racial, and gender lines. I see it among my students who struggle with motivation but are otherwise highly attuned to the injustices of a text. Chemical pollution could play a part, diet might be a factor, but the virtual world seems like a volume knob here, an accelerant. They compare themselves to others, or read of the latest tragedy, and the anxiety and depression interferes with sleep, and sleeplessness worsens mental health. Too, they live at the crosscurrents of societal ills, leaving them adrift.

Like the students I teach, my kids have developed strategies. Some combination of medication and therapy helps. My son has loved finding crawling things since he was young. He can find herps most anywhere they can be found, including venomous and endangered ones. He participated in a research project to identify a distinct line of salamander, the Blacksburg, *Plethodon jacksoni*, although the relentless calculation and lab work killed some of the joy of being a "kid in the woods." For my daughter, art, music, books, and writing do the trick. So do dancing and laughing with friends. I dropped her off for her first year of college at the University of Virginia two weeks after the Unite the Right rally in Charlottesville and despite that inauspicious start to her college career, she thrived and won a fiction award when she graduated. Bringing them on hikes, on canoe or camping trips, I hoped that basic competency in nature, a sense of wonder, might instill confidence, insulate them from the worst, but nature is no panacea.

Once on a canoe trip on the South Fork of the Potomac, the Smoke Hole Run, we shared the morels and the trout Sam and I had caught with an older boater who found ramps (wild leeks). We talked while staring at the mélange sizzling on a cast iron skillet in a smoky fire. "They have your values," he said, talking about the paths of his grown children. But parents eventually learn there are countless other streams and tributaries that flow into their kids, and that they may not be spared.

After a week on the river, I had shed much of the stress and frustration that builds in the day-to-day. The foam I see on the river can mesmerize, but it also makes me think of the foaming at the mouth when angry, like the river churning after a wrathful rapid. I have had no reason to seethe or be cross out here, save for missing the fruit stand. And the only person I might be comparing myself to is Hoff, who did the trip over one hundred years ago. Earlier in the year, I was passed over for a research award, which brought up a layer of resentment about which I was not proud. Jealousy, professional or otherwise, can be like shampoo foam: a little can be helpful to motivate you but too much and it stings your eyes and mouth.

Dry mouth was a lingering effect of the injury to my carotid artery. A stroke is basically a loss of liquid flow, so I stayed hydrated, keeping a bottle close, filling it with boiled river water in the evening and letting it cool overnight.

I am sometimes still overwhelmed by what happened, or the way we have trashed our planet, though I am also heartened by those (Jake, Ruth) who clean it. And I seem to have an overwhelming urge to see it before it is gone—or I am. "Beauty and terror," the poet Rainer Maria Rilke writes. Let them happen to you. "Just keep going."

Keep going I do. I knew this trip would challenge me, and that I would perhaps "find myself" in a challenge, but I wasn't out here to test my limits, to grind out long miles, or complete the journey in the Fastest Known Time (FKT), where people create endurance records. Growing older, one learns a bit more about accepting limits, adjusting them without embarrassment or regret.

The late Harold Deal lived somewhere near here. Along with other canoes, he designed Dave Simon's boat, the Mohawk Shaman, but he wouldn't sell it to Dave until he was ready. It had a hull designed to carve and corner when leaned aft, spin if the paddler leaned back. Deal made a name for himself by canoeing the whole two hundred miles of river in forty hours without sleeping. Not for me, but I was certainly at a point where I was straining, shoulders and arms sore. Burn in the trapezius. Channel strength.

≈ ≈ ≈

At Old Sow Island, the map said the channel was right, but left looked the better option. Letcher said there was a small gravel bar, and that passage is clear in the channel closest to the island. There was a rock ledge downstream, in the right channel, extending into the middle channel, large standing waves in the center channel.

When he entered Raubsville, Hoff noted the water had become clear again. In Easton it had been foul with "coal and sewage." He wrote that it takes "seven miles for a stream to purify itself"—by what scientific method I do not know. Or it is not polluted in the first place.

A guy from Carpentersville "lost the biggest smallmouth of my life." We can always put our losses in perspective. Things could always be worse. His daughters Maddie and McKenzie with their mom were fixing a rope swing, adding a stick to hold on to. The girls chased after Sully. They had to leave their lab pup home because he would jump off the boat. A country song played on their speaker about how it had been a "hell of a year." It sure had been. I thought of the one by the Mountain Goats, about making it "through this year, if it kills me." Two years for me, but who is counting?

At Riegelsville, I floated under a two-cable suspension bridge, built by Trenton's Roebling brothers, surely one of the most picturesque on the river. Cars crossed and the slowdowns I recognize. Hurry up while you have the bridge to yourself—slow down in the narrow passage when another car comes in the opposite direction.

Near Holland, I saw an eagle, and an osprey took a run at it. It did it again three or four more times, while the eagle ruffled some feathers, raised a wing, but then took off for a less exposed tree.

Was I ever bored? I like John Graves's answer in *Goodbye to a River*, about how there is merely not enough river. "You're no more bored with the sameness of your days and your diet and your task than a chickadee is bored, the passenger on the sunny bow, or a catfish; each day has its fullness, bracketed by sleep."

At Cook Creek, more kids played in the water. This was the site of the Durham furnace, which produced iron from 1698 until 1908. Robert Durham, who operated the furnace, developed the famous Durham boats used by Washington in his 1776 crossing downstream.

Birds fighting above weight, youthful splashing, blast furnaces, revolutionary marches—keep moving. Oh, and more mergansers out cruising.

≈ ≈ ≈

At Upper Black Eddy and Milford, I thought I might go ashore. Walk around. And using the rule I had devised about access, Milford won out. The Bridgerton Inn looked pretty charming, with a patio overlooking the river. Some day in the future, a luxury tour of the Delaware, with it and the Black Bass down in Lumberville, or the Lambertville Station, but for now, continue the minimalist one.

I stopped in the Milford Market, a small grocery/wine store with a deli in the back. It's a classic deli I recognize from my youth: slice the meat on the stainless circular blade, pile it on a bun. I ordered the Black Eddy, a black forest ham hoagie. That and a Lagunitas IPA to go, with pickle. This would make a great dinner at camp.

Where would I camp? I was entering a section of the river more private and developed, passing through historic towns, formerly stops on the canal or railroad. I knew there were public sites farther down near Bull's Island.

At the Frenchtown bridge, I briefly considered heading up to the upscale Frenchtown Inn bar, but I was wearing basically the same clothes

I put on a week ago: sandals, bathing shorts, and a quick-drying (but odor-trapping) top. People on the river basically wear the same uniform. Maybe that's why everyone on the river is so friendly, the usual markers of class and distinction erased. Up there, at the site of an old foundry, is Sunbeam Lenape Park, which the city renamed after the 2018 journey. ("Sunbeam" is a former name of the city.) When I joined them in 2022, the Lenape Nation held a treaty signing at the park. The town turned out with boxes of pizza, fresh beets, and lettuce locally grown. Over the years, the LNPA has built more and more friendships up and down the river. Jim Beer would point out a house—"they fed us hot dogs." And at Skinners Falls, a woman named Cynthia Nash, from a historic place called Innisfree (like in the William Butler Yeats poem), joined us on the bank at lunch, wanted to cook us a meal. Next time.

From Titusville, I have ridden my bike to Frenchtown on the towpath, so I was entering something like the familiar zone. The writer Elizabeth Gilbert lived here, and I remembered seeing from the bike the pink Italianate Victorian house she used to live in. When she put it on the market, Gilbert made a chatty video tour, selling "for no particularly rational reason except for that I love moving." You could eat, pray, and buy the house for about a million. It was built in 1869 by Joseph Reading, a governor and author himself of his travels in Gabon.

I hoped to get a peek at what resembled a widow's walk, the attic Gilbert turned into a library in the sky, or "skybrary." Hand-carved shelves resemble a tree house with secret hiding places. A king-size "napping bed" is tucked in a corner, with views of the river and surroundings, original ceiling beams, hip roof, a flight of stairs leading to the intimate aerie. The skybrary is 1,400 square feet, the size of my current house, but I had to hand it to her: had I written a bestseller made into a movie, I might also want to build a sanctuary for my books (and naps).

If I see the skybrary poking out of the trees, maybe I will walk up to the building, say hi to Liz, fellow writer. I hadn't eaten my sandwich yet and was maybe paddling on fumes. I saw a group parked out on a reef and thought of asking them.

A little farther down, another group, maybe they are local and would know. It would make good conversation anyway. Before I could ask, a young man in a white tank sitting half in the water called at me.

"You fish? You got fish in dere?"

"Not fishing today. Just paddling." The fishing rod I brought with me never made it out of the tube. "I'm headed to camp." One of the younger ones translated. They are ten in all, with two young kids.

"Food?"

I declined. "I have a sandwich." A Black Eddy to be precise.

"We got chicken. You want chicken? You want drink?"

Hmm. Why not? I steered the canoe in, dragged it up, and took a seat on the rocks.

Very soon, I held a Johnnie Walker Black with ice in a red plastic cup. Yari, short for Yarica, if I caught the name right, brought it to me, wearing cut-offs and a black tank, a cross in her necklace. The others told me their names and I wanted to write them down, but there was that Scotch on the rocks—literally.

Sully was glad to be out of the boat. She found a pork chop bone, gnawed it. I was too tired, and comfortable, to take the choking hazard away. I started toward her, but she ran, as if a game. Then she ran more, making figure eights, faster and tighter loops, her back legs under the front ones, turning, spinning, dog joy. *Eat, Play, Love.*

Yari came back from the cooler, the camp at the bank, with a plate full of chicken legs, barbecued, and a cold Corona. I was making figure eights now myself, internally. Sully had her own plate, a full breast it looked like. I sipped my JW.

We talked a little, or tried to.

"You speak Spanish?" The one who asked about the fish asked this. He seemed to be in charge, though there was also an older man, possibly a father, back by the coolers on the bank, wearing nice jeans and not swimming.

"I studied it in school," I said, but I can't say that in Spanish at the moment. "Salud," I offered, raising my plastic cup.

I asked the chief where they were from. He said from the Bronx. I was trying to determine where they were originally from, but like the Russians from New Jersey, the Orthodox Jews from the camp, they just wanted to be American. That was their identity. Make America a melting pot again.

Chief is probably in his early twenties. I tried some Spanish to explain my trip but also sought help from the younger boy, maybe a brother, probably in middle school.

"Why you do that?" he asked. If not for the language barrier, it might have been a version of *are you going through something?*

"I just wanted to see it. I grew up about twenty miles from here and have about twenty-five miles to go." The answer seemed to satisfy him.

"Why here and not the beach?" I asked him.

"I hate the beach. Too salty." He was fully in the shallow water now, crawling around the rocks, slurping the river and dribbling it back out.

Around this time, a helicopter landed just downstream from us in a riffle to the right of an island. It splashed down slowly, touched bottom, created ripples with the blades, paused, and then took back off. Some kind of landing practice?

"I've never seen that," I said.

"Neither have I," said the younger boy.

They have no idea of my recent history with helicopters, and the whole scene was more than a bit strange. Spying on us? Has one come for me? Nonsense. That was all in the past. I don't want to do that again. Have another sip of your Scotch-while-sitting-on-the-rocks.

They smoked a little from a hookah and the woman in a colorful print dress put the music on, smiling.

The kids kept splashing, and one of them smashed a glass bottle on a rock, using it like a hammer. It shattered, and I worried about their bare feet, but Yari stayed calm, admonished some, cleaned up the green shards. I joined her in the effort.

The young girl just went back to playing, possibly with her sister or cousin, and as dusk fell, I started to see who was with whom as they paired up. They sat on one another, swayed a little to the music, and one dripped water on her lover's head. She kissed his neck, he whispered something in her ear. *Eat, Dance, Love.*

They invited me back to the trees, as it was grilling time, even though I had just eaten their chicken. The woman in a colorful dress called me "Mister Señor," a redundancy they laugh at, even though I told them my name. They started a charcoal fire in a foil pan, handed me a second Corona, and a second Johnnie Walker, a healthy pour. There was a foil pan more of chicken to put on these coals. More food and drink.

The Italian phrase Gilbert learns is *dolce far niente*, or sweet doing nothing. But I was starting to think about camp. Also, I was thinking about their drive, and my canoe-paddle while intoxicated. I certainly could not make it back to the Bronx, but maybe driving was the older gentleman's job.

I stayed for a while, warmed by their fire, and company, but then made the gratitude sign, which I think is universal, as close as it is to a prayer. "Gracias," I said. Five or six years of Spanish and all I can remember are "health" and "thanks."

At Lambertville, the next town down, Hoff and company debated camping on the slope or continuing homeward. The question was decided for them when they reached the bridge. A crowd of fellow Park Island canoeists was waiting for them with food and good cheer.

I had good cheer too, though no escort. Just below Frenchtown is a cluster of about a dozen islands that occupy about two and a half river miles. Marshall Island was once called Man-of-War Island because the tall trees looked like masts of a battleship.

Night was falling but I still had enough light to pick my way through a narrow ribbon and tall trees, secluded. My mother went to Girl Scout camp on one of those, and my grandfather, her father, worked at one of the camps.

The water was swift, easy paddling, pick a channel and coast. The river looked faintly luminous, metallic. It might have been the booze, but this felt like the best part of the trip so far: gliding through the dark woods on the narrow river. I thought about who would play me in the movie should my book make it big, my Julia Roberts, and might have let out a little squeal of delight at the wonder of it all. *Eat, Paddle, Laugh.*

Gilbert offered a running gag of alternative titles but settled on the monosyllabic trio as working best. The jokes serve to "fumigate" sincerity, writes Rachel Cusk, "allay any suspicion the writer is taking herself too seriously." At the end of one island, when I found what seemed a pretty good place to camp, I could not compress my experience into her three-word mantra. Eat sandwich, sip beer, set up tent, love where you are.

My ties to the spiritual are somewhat tenuous, but the ritual of these evenings, the pattern of put up and take down, load and launch, along with the rhythm of paddle and water, the swoosh along the sides of the hull, felt like a very spiritual and sacred endeavor. It bore me thus far, reborn.

Before Gilbert takes off on her journey, she describes breaking down on the bathroom floor and talking to God (in any denomination) directly for the first time. She doesn't want to be married anymore, and in her despair, she asks God what to do. In asking, she stopped crying, preparing for an answer. The one she heard? "Go back to bed, Liz."

It was her own voice, but one calmer and more loving than the one usually ringing inside her head. She is surprised to feel better. I have heard people pan this moment in her book, but like the jokes over the titles, it is tongue-in-cheek: both a recognition that nothing would change right then and there, at least until some rest, and the beginning of an exploratory dialogue with bigger questions.

I had parked the boat on some cobble, pulled it up in case the rains came and the water rose. Then I grabbed the duffle with my tent and sleeping bag and walked to what seemed like a good spot. It was dark now, so I put on my head light. Either because of the slippery, mossy rocks, or because of the Johnnie Walker, I wobbled over. Then I pulled the crinkly tent from the bag and bent the poles into a dome.

I am usually not one prone to prayer, but there inside my cozy home, I thought of the gratitude I had for the chance to do this trip, for this particular island and spot, and for the recent generosity and kindness of my friends upstream. Lying down, staring up at the sky through the mesh, I thought something like "I hope I'm never too old for tents," which was close enough to a prayer. I faintly heard a voice speaking back: "Go to bed, Mister Señor."

The Uhlerstown-Frenchtown Bridge, built in 1931 on piers built in 1844.

FLOOD

Day 8—Frenchtown to Titusville
162–143

Before I listened to the voice, I texted my kids, some friends—twenty miles to home! I don't think it counted as drunk texting, but I did leave the phone on overnight. It had just 10 percent of battery—not bad for a week's work (with a back-up battery pack), but now none. I wanted to check the weather, see where the storm was, see who had texted back.

The weather I could check the old-fashioned way, by peering outside the tent. A pale sky rose above the treetops.

I felt a little shaggy, but also had the sense that I was close, no matter the weather. And despite my prayer last night, a bed would feel good, a shower too.

I never finished my beer, took only a bite of my sandwich before wrapping it back up in the white butcher paper. It would make a good breakfast, possibly even lunch. I boiled river water for coffee and sat on my stool. Just as I took a sip, I spied an eagle in the trees on the Pennsylvania side. It double-pumped and was off. A good omen. Some balance restored.

I took down the tent one last time. As much as I was looking forward to sleeping in a bed that night, I was also beginning to feel like I didn't want to leave the river.

With the boat packed, Sully jumped aboard. We had our routine down by now. She liked to stay on land until the last minute, but she also liked going wherever I was. Early in the trip, I had to give her a lift to entice her into the boat. She would give me a *do I have to?* look. By now, just a tap on the gunwale and she was inboard.

I paddled into the current, enjoying the islands by daylight. At the island nearby was a sign for Treasure Island. Up until 2006, it had been the nation's oldest continuously operated Boy Scout camp, since 1913. The flood in 2005 damaged many of the buildings. The Scouts spent over a million dollars restoring them, upgrading electrical work, but a flood in 2006 wiped out those efforts. The grounds sat unused until 2018 when a family bought the island, and a group of volunteers, former campers, is bringing scouting back.

The name may have come from the Robert Louis Stevenson novel, or from E. Urner Goodman, who is believed to have said upon visiting in 1912, "this island is a treasure." Goodman, from Philadelphia, founded the Order of the Arrow here, a kind of honor society of scouts. He was influenced by Ernest Thompson Seton and his Woodcraft Indians program. (Also, the traditions and secrecy of the Freemasons.) Too, he knew that the Lenape once inhabited the island. With assistant director Carroll A. Edson, they created imagery (such as turtles) and ceremonies borrowed from Lenape traditions. Those who completed the camp became members of the Unami Lodge. The full original name for the organization used Lenape dialect, Wimachtendienk Wingolauchsik Witahemui (Brotherhood of Those Who Serve Cheerfully), or just Wimachtendienk, "Brotherhood." The Order of the Arrow (OA) is still referenced as WWW on lodge patches. According to Phillip Deloria in *Playing Indian*, the OA was "based on a loose interpretation of *Hiawatha* and the novel *The Last of the Mohicans*." Inductions of new OA members at Treasure Island involved meeting around bonfires in "ritual Indian costume."

I toured the island with the volunteers and several in the Lenape Nation, and they were working together on appropriate, rather than appropriated, ceremonies and regalia. Girls were now welcomed into Boy Scouts, and those nonbinary, at least here, were welcomed as well. Before my time with the LNPA, I wondered if there would be "pretendians," those claiming heritage or appropriating cultural elements, but did not find that to be true. I met Marc Strong on the trip, who came from Denver by way of Nebraska. His ancestry was part Lakota but his grandmother was Lenape. He had never seen the home waters of her people—diaspora reunited with homeland. He saw no pretending either. Just people finding a purpose and connection. So were we all.

Past the island, I came upon a giant floating barge, anchored, bedecked with grills, condiments, and other food-service equipment.

Free BBQ Meal with Every Tube Rental
Delaware River Tubing, Inc. (Hatfield Meats)
(on the New Jersey Side)

When I called Gary Letcher before my trip, telling him I would be looking for stories on the river, he told me about Rick Lander and Ruth Jones but also Greg Crance. Greg was the "famous Delaware River hot dog man," owner of Delaware River tubing, but he died in May of that year at fifty-six, due to Covid. His sons were taking over the business.

Crance had battled New Jersey's Department of Environmental Protection for the right to operate his tubing business. He also lost concession agreements that allowed them access to the river from state parks. The website said they were closed in 2021 because of this dispute over access.

It seemed they owned this island, Adventure Island. A P. T. Barnum–style promoter, Crance would say, "You can have as good or better experience than going to a private island in the Caribbean."

Just past the island, another tubing business, one of the largest, Point Pleasant on the Pennsylvania side (now Bucks County River Country). They stacked tubes in blue, red, yellow, and green chutes, collected by color. They looked like Skittles separated into piles.

For a summer job, I worked at Abbott's Marine, downstream in Titusville. Here was our competitor in the tubing world. Our tubes were plain black inner tubes, hot in the sun. They would pick up grime and dust, and people would come back even dirtier after a day on the river, a rash under the arms from scraping the rubber while paddling, happy nevertheless.

Rocks have been taken out of the Point Pleasant Bridge piers, whole chunks, from the 1955 flood. The bridge is no more.

≈ ≈ ≈

Here, on the morning of January 10, 1983, a pickup rolled down River Road and into the historic village of Point Pleasant. In it was the construction crew hired to excavate the foundation of a water pumping station near the banks of the Delaware River. The truck was repulsed by more than two thousand citizen-activists who had been organized by Del-AWARE Unlimited, Inc., a grassroots environmental group, with help from its dollar-a-year consultant, the late Abbie Hoffman, renowned for his role in leading anti-war protests in the 1960s, then residing in Bucks County. Many had been camped at the site for weeks, waiting. They formed barricades with handmade stone walls, with their bodies, and their cars, hoping to turn back the construction equipment and block the diversion of Delaware River water to feed suburban sprawl and to cool the twin nuclear reactors of the Limerick power plant being built by the Philadelphia Electric Company (now PECO).

The scenario was repeated a day later, as the heavy equipment approached the activists' encampment from another direction, but this time, court order in hand, helmeted state troopers disbursed the protesters, arresting some of them. The pattern of resistance and arrests would continue for days, garnering national attention.

The mass display of civil disobedience was the culmination of more than three years of organizing, advertising, politicking, educating, and protesting, aimed at thwarting the construction of a multimillion-dollar water supply project. The system consisted of a pumping station to be built in Point Pleasant and transmission pipes leading to a reservoir to be erected nearby. Up to ninety million gallons of water daily would be drawn from the river and pumped overland to the reservoir, and from there, discharged into two Delaware tributaries: Neshaminy Creek and Perkiomen Creek. About half of the water would go to suburban communities in Bucks and Montgomery counties, and the rest to the Limerick nuclear power plant, as back-up coolant.

They carried signs: "Save the River, Dump the Pump," "No Need, Just Greed," "No De-hydration without Representation." Some sat down and blocked the vehicles. One protester climbed up on the mobile crane. Another handcuffed herself to a truck.

Although Del-AWARE participants had varied and sometimes multiple motives for their actions—antinuclear, antidevelopment, or natural resource protection being the most common—they spoke with one voice of their affection for the river. The organization invoked the imagery of the American Revolution, viewing its mission to stop the pump as democracy in action, underdog citizen-activists fighting for their cause.

Hoffman was among them, better known as a member of the Chicago Seven, the group of activists who went on trial for leading anti-war demonstrations that culminated in rioting at the 1968 Democratic National Convention. Hoffman was well rehearsed in the art of political theater: he helped "levitate" the Pentagon, dumped cash onto the floor of the New York Stock Exchange, and nominated a pig (Pigasus) for president in 1968.

While the Point Pleasant pump began life as part of a water supply and flood control system in the 1960s, when such public works projects were common, it would ultimately become operational in 1989 while the Tocks Island project would be decommissioned. Why? For one, visibility. The pump would not dramatically alter the course and flow of the river, like a dam, nor would it displace people like Ruth Jones or Nancy Shukaitis. Also, the pump was funded through a public-private partnership, so it was hard to resist on public policy grounds alone. But perhaps most importantly, timing. Del-AWARE began organizing nearly fifteen years after grassroots groups began questioning Tocks Island.

The 1980s saw the landslide election of Ronald Reagan and a backlash against the federal role in resource protection and public land management, led by grassroots groups from the West, and couched either in terms of states' rights, the so-called "Sagebrush Rebellion," or "wise use"—as opposed to preservation—of natural resources. "Wise use" was coined by Gifford Pinchot, but the doctrine espoused by Reagan's interior secretary, James Watt, promoted commercialization of resources on public land and resisted regulation of private land. While the rhetoric of "wise use" may have echoed Pinchot and early conservationists' measured approach to managing natural resources, the Watts/Reagan approach held a hard line on the commercial use of the public's land. That approach trickled down (one of Reagan's favorite metaphors) to Harrisburg.

I remember some of the protests. I was a sophomore in high school, still trying to figure out where I fit in socially more than politically, but I knew I was on the side of the river—literally.

≈ ≈ ≈

Just below here, I ran the wing dam at Bull's Island. Two concrete piers with a center passage impound water for the Delaware and Raritan Canal. A man had walked out on one of the concrete wings and stood on one of the piers, waving me through. Letcher calls it a "precipitous drop-off," but Sully and I are old hands and paws at this by now.

The D&R Canal begins here, a feeder canal or water conduit to the main stem, which ran from Bordentown to New Brunswick, connecting to the Raritan River and then out to the Atlantic. The idea goes back to William Penn in 1676—Philadelphia to New York across New Jersey.

While this section of the canal was not built primarily for boats, they did travel here, often crossing in Lambertville, above Wells Falls, to the Delaware Canal on the Pennsylvania side, connecting the communities up and down the river.

Below the rapids, I could raise up off the seat and peer into the canal, several feet above, held by a drystone wall. The wall was built and the canal dug by Irish immigrants. A deadly epidemic swept through the labor camps in 1832 and many workers were buried here in unmarked graves, with one mass grave at Bull's Island. The stonework is hand-laid, precision masonry, still solid and retaining water, a testament to their craftsmanship.

Then the Lumberville-Raven Rocks pedestrian bridge, another Roebling. The famous Black Bass Hotel perched above on the bank, green umbrellas closed on the stone patio—some other time.

Paddling on, I saw a few big houses, stately and modern. One of my first jobs was working for a kitchen contractor. The owner had renovated our kitchen and somehow I signed on to help. He often worked in the high-end homes near here and was savvy. Drive the beat-up van to the estimate. Makes you look both needy and authentic. I did little but fill nail holes and install hardware on cabinets.

One house is plate glass, cantilevered. The upstairs bathroom has a view on the water, but I have a view in. Someone has left the toilet seat up.

At Lambertville/New Hope, more flood of memory. In high school I used to take my girlfriend to Thomas Sweet's in New Hope for ice cream. Sweet cream and strawberry for her, cookies and cream for me. Good breakfast up there in Lambertville, at the Full Moon and Sneddon's, a classic lunch counter.

I decided to walk around some. But before I did, I paid a visit to the person sitting in the bridge tender booth. With a window on the bridge, their job is basically to watch over things, make sure no large trucks try to travel over these narrow bridges. The old, wooden one was wiped out in a 1903 flood. This one was built in 1904, so travel is slow.

My father earned a degree in business and found his way into partnership in an electrical supply company. A terrific salesman, he was quick with a joke and hearty laugh after, no matter how funny. He was eminently practical, liked doing and getting things done. Such qualities earned him a role on the township council, then mayor, then director of the Mercer County Improvement Authority, and ultimately, director of the Delaware River Joint Toll Bridge Commission, which oversaw these bridges and their employees. I'm not sure exactly what his position entailed, although he liked inspecting job sites, always in polished shoes and a suit, signature high-water pants, floods. He worked one of his first jobs at a men's clothier, DiIorio's haberdashery, believing the clothes made the man. I once asked him what was the secret to his success? Basically, "I talk with people and make them laugh."

It had been twelve years since he died (melanoma, which is why I keep up with the sunscreen), but out of curiosity, I had to ask. Did the guard in charge know my father?

Keith Culbertson did not directly, but his wife did. She worked at the insurance company where he was on the board of the directors, another post. My father was famous for helping people secure employment, and Keith was due for a bridge tender job thirteen years ago. He was now happily employed.

"I didn't know your dad well." Among others working at bridges, he heard "nothing but good things. An awesome guy."

I told him what I was up to, paddling this river, and said thanks. "Enjoy the metropolis of Lambertville," he said, in the sarcasm of my people.

Only from where I have been of late could it be called a metropolis. I have walked this street many times, yet after a week on the river, it looks strange. The jewelry stores had fine displays in the window, bracelets and rings encased in velvet. Several stores sold polished antiques.

My father and I had our clashes, mainly over clothing style or my not putting something away. I preferred the worn-in look and could be forgetful about replacing a tool right away, which didn't seem a cardinal sin at the time. I would get around to it. But I do now, hearing him in my head: *put something away and you'll know where to find it*. He lived by simple maxims, but I wanted complexity, not platitudes. Still, it was hard for him to complain. I hooked good grades and mostly stayed out of trouble.

At the Lambertville Station, I checked out the menu: a salmon gyro, oysters, mahi mahi. Looked good, but I was not dressed for it. And no local shad, which was not in season anyway. From the bridge tender's booth, you can see where each year they haul in the shad, which gives rise to a festival.

≈ ≈ ≈

For forty years the town of Lambertville has held a shad festival here, part celebration of the fish, part street fair. From the bridge, I looked down on the Lewis Fishery, on twenty-four-acre Holcombe Island, just upriver from the bridge. Sully and I had stopped to walk around on the island. It's the last commercial fishery on the upper Delaware, although "commercial" may be misleading. It implies there is money to be made. Shad fishing used to be big business. But by the 1940s, pollution from factories had depleted the oxygen in the river and reduced the catch to single digits. In the early fifties, Fred Lewis caught no shad at all. Most of the other fisheries closed. He urged state authorities to clean up the river. The shad began to return in the 1960s, and Lewis, who died in 2004, partnered with researchers and state biologists, collecting samples, tagging fish, and recording hauls. His grandson, Steve Meserve, continues the tradition, but mostly to continue the tradition.

John McPhee wrote a book on shad and his admitted obsession with catching them, *The Founding Fish*, so named because while Washington's army may or may not have feasted on them at Valley Forge, he certainly fished for them at Mount Vernon. Shad was to Philadelphia as cod was to Boston, writes McPhee, and their return in the sixties is likely the result of the '55 flood. The flood waters "plucked millions of pumpkins off the floodplains and spewed them like birdshot far into the Atlantic." And when the floodwaters reached the filth and sludge of the pollution barrier near Philadelphia, "they scoured them out like a blown nose."

Shad, like salmon, are anadromous, returning from the sea to their fresh-water natal home. On spawning runs, they don't eat, surviving on fat, but will bat away colorful irritants known as shad darts. No one knows why, and they will just as likely ignore one or snap at it like an angry dog.

In the opening essay, "They're in the River," McPhee describes getting a call about the shad run. He and Ed Cervone fish off the fourth pier at this very bridge, in the shadow of what was Club Zadar, a disco that burned down. Club Zadar in its heyday was a cross section of New Hope: part punk meets gay meets tourist with a sprinkle of Princeton preppy and Philly yuppie mixed in. It was cavernous and dark and a great window ran the length of the club facing the river, but few people were there for the scenery—more the scene.

McPhee hooks into something but it fights for two and a half hours. Their wives call the bridge tender who shouts from the bridge their concern. You guys OK? They are not sure what's on—large rainbow from upstream? Striped bass? Catfish or carp? Maybe a shortnose sturgeon, that used to more frequently run these waters but are now endangered and rare. He nets a four-and-three-quarter-pound roe shad—not particularly remarkable in size but in fight. It stripped the gears of his reel.

Ed Cervone was a mentor at my first teaching job at the Pennington School. He was a Princeton grad, held a doctorate in psychology and made a career of helping students with dyslexia and other learning disabilities. "Doc" Cervone would finish the Sunday crossword in the faculty lounge during the break between classes. I once tried to use that association to ask McPhee either for a blurb or a reading. "Congratulations to Ed Cervone's anadromous mentee," he wrote, in declining, being notoriously shy about readings and reluctant to give blurbs.

In the appendix of the book, McPhee includes recipes for shad. One is from a master dart maker, Armand Charest: "You take a shad. You put it in a pressure cooker with a brick. You cook it for eight hours. Then you throw away the shad and eat the brick."

≈ ≈ ≈

I could see the mansard roof of the Bucks County Playhouse, which occasionally brings in national acts, and near here, when I was in high school, a TV news anchorwoman, Jessica Savitch, drowned in the Delaware Canal. She and Martin Fischbein dined at Chez Odette and made a wrong turn. Fischbein was driving; Savitch was in the back seat with her dog.

At Lambertville Falls, I got out to scout on the wing dam from the left side. Hoff and crew carried over the small dam to the other side, breaking bread with members from the club. He described the rocks between the dam, a diabasic ledge, and a "treacherous foamer" below. Letcher said it was the most severe rapid on the river, and the only one measured above class II. It's "two plus," but from where I stood on the concrete, looked three-ish.

I made my own wrong turn here once when about fourteen. With a friend from down the street, we borrowed a neighbor's aluminum canoe, and, with no particular destination in mind, paddled up the canal. We pulled hand over hand through the beams under the canal bridges, thick in creosote and cobwebs. And then, reaching Lambertville, had the bright idea that the river would bear us more easily home. We had PFDs, knew the reputation of the falls, but how bad could it be? We ran it without scouting. The water was up and we swamped in the first wave, still wearing our street clothes. We floated with the overturned canoe to the gravel ramp below where we emptied it and paddled home, drenched, crazy, happy, a little astonished at the boldness of our act.

Since then, I've tubed it, kayaked it, and once rode a motorized raft up through it, so it was somewhat familiar, but still impressive and intimidating. While eating the rest of my Black Eddy sandwich on one of the large tree trunks brought in by a flood, I saw a main rock in the center that was to be avoided with some haystacks three or four feet high. I chose the left side, a bit of a sneak route, and marked the V to get me there. A curtain of flume poured over the downstream edge of submerged stone. The air was thick with the texture of spray: silty, gritty, a fine froth. The roar brought a line into focus.

With Sully back in the boat, we hit our marks but even the sneak took us into big black rocks that had to be avoided. That rock is diabase, the hardest in the world, which makes up Goat Hill and nearby Belle Mountain. It mostly saved the hills from the plow and bulldozer but was mined in quarries nearby to make the Belgium block of historic streets, Fells Point in Baltimore, Germantown Avenue in Philadelphia. John Hart, a signer of the Declaration of Independence, hid in these, the Sourland Mountains, until the Continental Army's capture of Trenton, when he returned to his Hopewell Valley farm.

The hull hit a wave and pushed us off target. I ruddered hard right, swept back left so as not to overcorrect, slipped between two massive boulders on river left, just barely squeezing through.

≈ ≈ ≈

Around the bend is the ramp where we had emptied the swamped canoe when younger, by the Golden Nugget flea market, and beyond it Bald-pate Mountain (once called Canoe Mountain). According to Sally Galla-gher, in her 1873 history of Lambertville, there used to be a stone tavern just below the falls. "This tavern was also a great place for card-playing, drinking and fisticuff fighting."

As Gallagher describes it, one night after the game, some local boys procured a ewe, led him up the roof and shoved him down the chimney. The blackened sheep gave a loud "bah," sprang for the door, upset the card table, and "struck consternation in the hearts of the gamesters," who fled for their lives. Ever after, witnesses believed they had indeed seen his "Satanic Majesty" materialized, "for they had a glimpse of his hoofs and horns."

After the flea market, Belle Mountain, where I learned to ski. It was a small hill with a rope tow and a chair lift, the "big hill" and an inter-mediate one, plus one "bunny" slope. The rope tow would chew up your gloves, and if you were with somebody, the chair was always better. Good days there, nights too, skiing under the lights. My friend Dave's parents parked their motor home across the street, but we wanted hot chocolate in the warming hut, not the camper. On a trip there in fifth grade, Dave told me he kissed Linda on the chair. He had an older sister I had a crush on, and he knew about such things. I should kiss my date too, said Dave. Was it a date? More like I'd be there and okay, she would be too. The girls were together as much as the boys were. I kept trying to build up the courage on the lift, if not by pole four then certainly by pole five, because after that it was time to raise the bar, keep ski tips up. On the next run, or the run after that, I finally did lean in, crossed a threshold, there in the dark treetops and high on a cable, weightless, a first kiss, a warm feeling better than hot chocolate. It was with Jamie, who was tomboyish, good on the kickball court, which mattered at one time, but was starting to matter less and less.

If I search on Google or Facebook, those portals that offer some satisfaction to the *what ever happened to* question, I learn that Dave worked for a while as a chef in Boulder, plays drums in a classic rock band, attended the wedding of his oldest son not long ago. His cover picture is of Ringing Rocks, near Upper Black Eddy. It's a field of angular boulders, and when struck they ring like a bell. Hoff had stopped there but I had passed. For him, they are "a collection of metallic boulders that emit ringing and even musical combinations of sounds upon being struck." Must have appealed to the drummer in Dave.

In pictures, the very same parents are there at the grandson's wedding. I can hear his mom calling him *Davit*. He wrote something cryptic a while back about the way we refer to chapters in our lives, new ones, as if things are supposed to get better. Sometimes they don't. And wouldn't it be nice if the person writing our book gave more notice when they were about to close one chapter and begin a new one?

Jamie transitioned from kickball to field hockey and golf in high school, and the golf seems to have stuck. A daughter, the oldest of three, graduated from college last spring. She poses with friends from travels to Ireland, Italy. The husband is mostly absent. In these pictures she is brightly, neatly dressed (my father would approve), smiling, but who knows? How much is the real us and how much is our screen avatar? The face-we-present-book.

Around another curve, the entrance to what was a kind of sacred site when growing up. We called it Monkey Island but others called it John's. Letcher has it as Keeler's Island, "left channel normally too dry for passage." Trees are down at the upstream end, brought in by a flood, and it is silted in. Around the other end, the entrance is wider. There used to be a rope swing here, tied high to a silver maple branch. The tree is gone but the slope is still silty, which made it an ideal spot for getting a running start and hang on. The bottom was silt too, not rock, so soft landing if you slipped off the rope.

A lot of good days here, sweet ones. Used to be nettles growing outside the silty area, what we called "itch weed." Japanese knotweed has moved in. We once rubbed the nettles on ourselves intentionally, soothed our burning skin with the river mud. We would swing out on the rope in circles, lob small mud balls at the swinger, which would stick to the belly in star prints. If you didn't laugh you held on. If you did, you fell into the water. Either way a winner.

With my friends Tim and Tom, we camped here. We thought we were sneaking a six-pack of Miller Lite out of a basement, but my dad caught us, pulled three from the plastic ring, sent us on our way. Tom later became Tomo, another drummer in a band, this one with a record label.

I once tubed this stretch with a group of co-teachers at the Pennington School, celebrating the end of the school year. We came around this bend and saw a couple making love on the rocky beach. We stayed quiet, not wanting to disturb, but then stood in the middle of the shallow river and began clapping.

Then a riffle, which we called Snuffy's, named for the roadside stand that used to be there, before it was the Fife and Drum, with a dock for boat visitors, and now an upscale Italian place, described in an online review as a "quaint BYOB with Mediterranean chow." Letcher calls the rapid Titusville Rift, which we never did. I wonder what other names are known to locals and not to maps.

I looked for the two rocks that signal the passageway through. I once hit somewhere in here, a loud underwater boom, bending the prop. My father hung these on a nail in the garage, a memorial to mistakes, at least the ones made on the river. I came to know this section, John's to home, very well. Each and every rock, reef, a map in my head, one I was reliving.

My father used to bring me up here when I was young, scouting for old railroad ties. When the railroad tracks were torn up, crews must have tossed the ties, and those would be recycled by my father into a riverbank protection system. Or at least a place to put some stairs leading down to the water's edge. To this day I scour the shoreline, as if looking for treasure, though more often now feathered flying jewels.

I worked for a time in the warehouse my father co-owned, sweeping floors with a large push broom and unloading trucks. By starting me young, he thought I might develop a taste for work and one day take on the business, but I rarely felt useful. More like someone other employees had to watch, take to lunch. In a world of uncertainty, it might be nice to have a path chosen for you, one swept clean, but he gave me an even better gift: a love for the river.

Here at Snuffy's, I once helped on a movie set, the making of the mini-series *George Washington*, with Barry Bostwick as George and Patty Duke Astin as Martha. Jaclyn Smith played the love interest, Sally Fairfax, and I hoped to get a glimpse of my favorite Angel. I ran errands, used the boat some for support, and my important job was to stand on the reef and swing some lanterns, signaling the coast is clear, a good time for the Durham boats to cross. Cut to special effects, including something resembling cornflakes thrown in front of a giant fan to make snow.

Just after the riffle the sky darkened some, clouds heaping and stacking, as if a rapid in a river.

Rivers are distilled clouds.

With about a half mile to home, I hit the worst headwind of the trip, as if something was keeping me from finishing, or holding us back. With the squalls Sully joined me in the rear, not on the black box, where she will sometimes perch, but the actual stern. With no weight in the bow, the gusts turned us around. And because the canoe acted like a sail when I tried to right the ship, I paddled backward for a while, pull rather than push.

Our family used to park a pontoon boat up here, pack a picnic or something to grill, float back home. To escape the wind, I steered over to the New Jersey shore, and by now, I have really entered the remembrance zone. I passed the boat ramp that I helped my father and others build when I was young, if by help you mean clear a few branches, swing on the vines. It is chained off but for people in the community and the Union Fire and Rescue, where my father was a volunteer and chief.

The ramp is a boat launch and a tubing one too. I came up here earlier in the summer with a woman I had connected with at the beginning of the year, in part through a writer of rivers, our friend John Lane. Her last name translates to "flooding river" and she is a writer and poet with an eye for beauty. We planned a trip to Maine to visit her former roommate, shake off some Covid cobwebs, and we stopped here, midway in our journey north. And what does one do with a woman one is interested in? One takes her tubing, of course. We floated and laughed and looked at treetops drifting by, feet and bottoms in the water. By the bank we spied a fox out for a sip staring back at us, all of us silent, awestruck. When you tube with someone, you might drift apart, so you reach out with hand or toe to hold them close.

In a tube, water caresses the body, like love. Like love, there is an eros to a river, a pull and force to it, that can cut new grooves through rock.

In "This Old Man," an essay for the *New Yorker*, the late Roger Angell writes that the biggest surprise of his life is "our unceasing need for deep attachment and intimate love." Everyone in the world, he writes, wants to be with someone. The longing, when it returns, stuns and alters us.

A first kiss when young, or on a chairlift, or now, is not without its awkwardness, or reticence. Yet in "Crocus Explains," the poet Stephen Dunn, a friend and former teacher of hers, says, "I've been known to risk everything. / . . . so be it. / Otherwise I'd be . . . / . . . forever waiting / for a sign that says, 'It's safe now.'" "Some of us just can't help ourselves," he continues, "a little warmth, and we're goners."

I felt turned around, and I didn't want it to end.

Just past the new ramp was the old one and a rock reef, what my son calls Snake Island, because he would find water snakes here. Neighbor David Earling has renovated what was the old fruit and vegetable canning place at the north end of town.

Remembrance zone constricts further, current of memory swifter. I know most of the houses and docks. What used to be the McDonalds' has a nice stone wall. Earling and Hoch—Mr. Hoch drove a golf cart in the parade with the word "commodore" on it. Deborah Maher sang opera, and the most rousing rendition of the national anthem. Rumor had it she taught Debbie Harry, from the band Blondie, to sing.

One summer, Ethan Hawke's mom lived in town, or he had bought her a place, circa *Dead Poets Society* (not that they ever die). He visited and some friends tried to pull him up on water skis but he had trouble and his suit started to fall off. Ha! He could act but could Mr. Hollywood water ski? My sister Gretchen was in the boat, coaching a little, taking pictures too. She has yet to auction embarrassing shots of Ethan.

Then what used to be the Delaware House, part inn for canal traffic, also former post office. My grandmother used to live in the front apartment. The Griffiths always had chickens before having chickens was a cool hobby.

I then rowed past the church I went to, though less and less as I got older. And next door, a ravine, where we played, and beyond it the graveyard where my grandfather, grandmother, and father are buried.

Then the Canes, good friends, new wall and patio—boats looking good. And what used to be the Kellys'. Tom would tube with a book in hand, sometimes a beer or cigarette in the other. Daughter Colleen, a year older than me, would sunbathe on the dock here. That might have held possibilities, but our mothers went to college together, which made us practically siblings.

Then the Millers' and I see it. There's no particular curve in the river here, but I know where I am by the distance to the bridge, the start of the small island across, the houses on the hill. The big ash tree is gone—they mostly all are—but the rock in the water is still there, the one we used to measure the river level, the one we absolutely could not budge when we removed other big rocks to clear out the swimming area and provide some bank protection.

Our dock was not in. Our neighbor down the street, Bob, usually puts it in and keeps his boat there, but Covid has thrown him and his back off. I would use the Millers' next door.

The blue-barreled dock sat on the landing, the one held up by our railroad-tie engineering, nearly fifty years strong. From here, the dock could be slid into the water with planks, ropes, and the help of other neighbors. There used to be a "dock day," one in the spring and one in the fall, where the guys would help each other lower or raise. Put in during spring when the water is up for summer use. Take out in winter to avoid ice floes, which would damage the homemade frames, though ice floes now are few and far between.

I am a little nostalgic for that community, though not for the conformity that sometimes came with it. Those with other interests, or hobbies, were mocked, their docks unmoved.

I stepped out of the boat, stiffly, and onto shore. The rocks have been rearranged by floods or ice, but the railroad-tie wall above is in good shape. There is a good deal of silt up here washed in from floods. The small shed that held our life jackets, fishing rods, water skis still stands. It's a replacement for the repurposed outhouse my father found floating down the river.

Ten days from my landing at my parents' home, the tropical depression will morph into hurricane Henri, Ida on the heels of it, and this will be underwater. The river will crest at 16.91 feet at the Washington Crossing

Bridge, putting it in the top ten for flood events. The '55 and 1903 floods still top the charts, 27.77 and 25.90 feet respectively. Third on the list was April of 2005 and fourth was June 29, 2006, at 22.5 feet. We were in Slovenia at the time of this last flooding for a friend's wedding and saw notice of it and an evacuation order here and in Trenton on international news. Our young children, then nine and eight, were staying with their grandmother, so it was a little disconcerting. But the bank is high here on the New Jersey side—the floodplain in Bucks County gets it worse. The '55 flood came to about the third or fourth step from the top, but never came into this section of town, though other houses, of course, did see devastation. One hundred people died in the basin.

That '55 flood was the product of two hurricanes, Connie and Diane, and saturation over a period of days. What made the flooding from Ida so bad was the intense rainfall. Three inches in an hour, as much rain in a day as they normally receive in a month. The river rose but the tributaries created problems as the creeks flooded, washing out streets and bridges.

Roger Miller, whose mom and dad were friends with my grandparents, has said to use the dock like it's your own. As I pulled in, he was inspecting from above.

"Thought I recognized a familiar face. Where'd you put in?"

"Hancock."

"Aw, that's a great trip. I've done it."

He went back to fixing up his family's place. My mother and father babysat him and his three siblings when they were young, they my sisters and me, and we the grandchildren, they ours, and so on.

He had recently cut the brush back on the bank, a job I used to do on our side. Memory thickets, gets cleared but keeps growing back. Or memories are those recirculating eddies. Or they are ripples on water, standing out in relief. They are sticks in the drift pile, wedging in. The journey home is always meandering, bendy. The yard looks smaller, the woods not nearly as tall and tamer. But the river, somehow, has grown. The abundance of it all floods the heart.

This was home, but I am experiencing past moments in present skin. The house on the hill is the same externally, but inside much has changed. After my mother and stepfather married, they renovated the inside, adding bathrooms to the upstairs and attic, expanding the kitchen, opening things up. It is much improved, but both the same and not quite the same.

I headed up the steps to street level. This is the river by which I have measured other rivers, the town other towns. From what I have learned, I might have stayed right here. Only then I wouldn't know that.

When my parents divorced, initiated by my father, it was hard to understand why anyone would want to leave this. It has occurred to me that my search for place, that most writing on the sense of place, is motivated by loss, or learning to value what is before us, deepening our appreciation.

I walked around to the back, climbed up the steps, and walked through the door just like always. My mother and stepfather were reading the newspapers. The river has borne me back home.

The Washington Crossing Bridge, built in 1904 on piers, 1834.

FALLS

Day 9—Washington Crossing to Trenton

143–136

From the bank above, I spied the inert boat down below, tied to the dock. A little rain had fallen, so some water pooled in the bottom, dirt and mud from the trip too, but otherwise it sat empty. In the pale morning light the gray-green river drifted under curling wisps of spray. On this final day I would leave the dog and gear behind for the last leg. I packed only a water bottle, a small carafe of coffee to place in my cup holder, and my dry bag with my camera, notebooks, and pen. I brought *Canoeing the Delaware*, the maps too—already tucked into the seat back—but mostly I knew the way.

The end would not be far, maybe seven more miles. My plan was to get out at a spot I scouted near Rotary Island. It was Park Island in Hoff's day, and that's why they were the Park Island Canoeing Association. Hoff said he and the Trenton canoeists regularly "unearthed" arrowheads, stone hatchets, and pottery shards on the island. A former neighbor, Kathy McGuire, who volunteered as an archivist with the

Trenton Public Library, and helped me find some information on Hoff, lives in the neighborhood across from the island, and assisted in finding a spot to take out.

Below that is the city of Trenton, the fall line, where the river meets the sea. Like Richmond on the James and Washington on the Potomac, cities along the East Coast grew where ship traffic could meet inland transportation and commerce, mills and factories could be built. It is where, as Indigenous people used to say, the river runs two ways. The rapids before are nothing too difficult, save for a mass of ledges on river right nearly impassable in low water, a dangerous hydraulic river left. Hoff took out at Park Island, so good enough for me as a place to finish. I scouted the site earlier with my septuagenarian shuttle mom.

The first thing I noticed when I sat in the boat and put my paddle to water was how light the boat was, so light I laughed. And the water in the early morning was calm, mostly glass. Under these conditions, I could go all the way to Cape May and Delaware Bay.

When I was younger, we headed mostly upstream, for practical reasons. Go up and you'll float back down. I know the way, but docks and their owners are a little less familiar downstream, though I still know most of them. This vast open space created something among us, something we shared. You might never go inside their home, but you saw neighbors on the river, or out on the street on their way there.

One of the first landmarks is the school on the hill. I went there from kindergarten through third grade. It closed not long after and now serves a special needs population bussed in. I used to be able to walk to school, only a short block. From my third-grade classroom window, I could look out on the river, even when Miss Judkins read to us from *A Wrinkle in Time*. Then it became the bus stop, and we were ferried to Bear Tavern, on the very road Washington and his army took to Trenton.

The school had a bell on top and when teenagers we figured out how to climb to a lower roof, scaling up a gutter. Then paw the shingles to the peak, clang the bell. Just to say we did it. Just to be heard.

In a classroom up there yet another origin of this trip. I remember watching a film, *Paddle to the Sea*, made in the year I was born, 1966. The Canadian canoeing legend, Bill Mason, directed it, based on the Holling C. Holling book of the same title, a Caldecott honoree in 1942. Both tell the story of a boy who carves a canoe with a wooden Native American as paddler. On the bottom the boy writes, "please put me back in the water. I am Paddle-to-the-Sea." The homemade craft starts in creeks, goes through lakes, past a sawmill, a plunge over a falls, by large seagoing ships, until it meets the ocean. It probably introduced me and a whole generation to the idea of a watershed.

Up there is where the Independence Day parade is always held, and because of our proximity to the crossing, its importance to the revolution, our small town goes all in. A jazz band and mummers from Philly, a drum or dancing corps from Trenton, a baby and bike parade for local kids, then fire trucks from the local fire company, Union Fire and Rescue, joined by the classic red of Hopewell, gray of West Trenton and Pennington.

Another origin: once in the parade, in the early seventies, I was dressed as clean air, with a gas mask; my sister Jennifer was clean water, in kiddie pool; and my other sister Gretchen was towed behind as population control, the number "two" crossed out on the float's sign, "three" children per family. Before the Clean Water Act of 1972, many rivers were environmental hazards. The Cuyahoga famously caught fire (multiple times). President Nixon vetoed the bill, but both the Senate and House overrode.

In high school I would engage in debates with my classmates over which was better, river or ocean. Many in my school, a mere five miles away, had little idea the river existed. In the late eighties in New Jersey, I thought I had a clear case. Syringes and garbage came in with the tides, washed up on the Jersey shore, the result of barges hauling out trash and dumping it. Out of sight, until washed back on the beach. That I swam in the river was considered gross. That I sometimes bathed in it, kept a bar of soap in a dish under the dock, utterly repulsive, made me unfit for society. But the Clean Water Act laws were on my side, and I had witnessed the water getting clearer, cleaner, and less polluted every year.

Not that it was always that way. Sewage used to be discharged from cities, consuming oxygen and suffocating fish. Hoff noted how the water near Easton was "foul with coal and sewage." In the worst places, that rotten-egg smell of hydrogen sulfide. To call attention to the water quality issues, in 1933 a group of canoe clubs collaborated on the Great Canoe Marathon. Ninety-four teams raced all the way from Easton to Trenton, people cheering from bridges and banks. The race was the brainchild of Harry Cudney of Hackettstown, who worked for the New Jersey Fish and

Game Commission. The river was dying—clots of wood pulp, heaps of oily scum, masses of dead fish. Cudney knew that before anything could be done to clean the river, people had to develop a concern that matched his own.

Water quality today is "good" north of Trenton and "excellent" above the Water Gap. In 1967 the Delaware River Basin Commission developed some of the most comprehensive standards in the nation. By the end of the eighties, the DRBC had spent over $1 billion on wastewater improvements.

Today, the entire two hundred miles of river is covered under a Special Protection Waters (SPW) program by the Delaware River Basin Commission, adopted in 1992, which monitors and aims to keep water quality above existing standards. Their motto is to "keep clean water clean," and they embarked on the program to preserve the already clean water in the river. John Yagecic, manager of water quality assessment, told me it is much easier, more cost effective, to "prevent impairment from happening in the first place." The program ensures that wastewater treatment is up to or above standards, that any new facilities won't harm water quality. Two main problem areas persist: chloride levels, likely due to road salt, and bacteria, which is a problem also in the headwaters, and is likely due to wildlife (deer, Canada geese). Yagecic told me an advantage the Delaware has over the Susquehanna is that there is not nearly as much agriculture in the watershed. The SPW regulations established the longest stretch of anti-degradation policy on any river in the nation.

As good as water quality was, Maya K. van Rossum, in charge of the Delaware Riverkeeper Network, wanted to see it better, especially in the estuary. Her riverkeeper group was running a "Dino in the Delaware" campaign, with billboards that said "Extinction Sucks" above an image of an Atlantic sturgeon, in existence for more than one hundred million years. They were overharvested especially for their caviar roe. Russian aristocracy prized the black delicacies, paying as much as $1,400 in today's dollars for a single female fish. During spring migration in the nineteenth century, some 360,000 fish thronged in brackish parts of the river. During Hoff's time, the caviar rush and overharvest was on. Today, there are fewer than 250 of them left.

For them to thrive, to be spared from extinction, they need more oxygen in the water. The current standard for dissolved oxygen in the estuary, where the sturgeon spawn, is about 3.5 milligrams per liter, set by the DRBC. Van Rossum wanted to see a standard nearly twice that, to pull these fish back from the brink. Dissolved oxygen is lower in the estuary, which can be warmer and contains salt water, but also because of sewage treatment. Getting to a higher standard would be a heavy financial lift, but van Rossum told me her riverkeeper organization was going to ask the DRBC, under their authority under the Clean Water Act, to raise it anyway, and if they would not, to petition the EPA.

≈ ≈ ≈

The paddling was light, but without the ballast, a little harder to keep Marge on the straight and narrow. Pull forward to about the hip, with a little twist and outward pressure at the end of the stroke, make the letter J, using the paddle like a rudder, checking the tendency to veer off center. Watch the vortices trail behind me.

At Trimmer Avenue, Hoff had a summer cottage, though I'm not sure which one. He bought the land from George Trimmer. Possibly the Swansons', or what was the Van Hises'. An article I found in the *Trenton Evening Times*, 1904, said that J. Wallace Hoff, secretary to the fire commission, and Mrs. Hoff are "summering" in Titusville. "Mr. Hoff has purchased a building plot and is now superintending the erection of a comfortable bungalow where he will while away the heated term. His place is along the river front and is a cozy and cool spot." His obituary was in 1922. "Although he had been in failing health, his death came as a shock to his family."

He was my age when he died.

The river here isn't wild but it is still dangerous. Somewhere in here a water ski fatality in the eighties. The boat owner's brother, home from army leave, crashed into a dock. The boater had to call the Union Fire and Rescue Squad of which he was a volunteer. There were several drownings when I was growing up, once a whole family when the father put the boat in reverse, took in too much water over the transom and sank. One late afternoon I watched my father, a former lifeguard, also a volunteer with the fire company, for many years its chief, pull a man out, drag him onto the boat, and administer mouth-to-mouth. The bloated man finally coughed up water, took in air. The thing that irked my father was not the bent railing, caused by dragging the man up and over, not the vomit that had to be cleaned up, but that the man never thanked him, showed any form of gratitude, then or after, for saving his life.

After Trimmer, a house displays a Hopewell Valley Historical Society sign, marking the original house date and owners on the street, Theodore and Charity Vannoy, 1865, though I'm not sure how we're related. Some closed up the space between the *n*'s and some kept it. That marker is one of the only on the street with the woman's name on the sign, so maybe her name was on the deed too.

Then Grant Street, where Jim Abbott, a.k.a. River Jim, lived. He had Abbott's Marine, boats and canoes, where I worked as a teenager. I was once the drummer boy in the Christmas pageant, but the program had my name as "Risky." I was Risky to him forevermore, including when he took us canoeing upstream.

Jim was both the main rescuer on the river and the man in charge of dock day. He had a winch on his Jeep and would use it to lower and raise the heaviest of the docks. While the others did the heavy lifting and hard labor, the joke to Jim above, finger on the switch, "how's your thumb Jim? Tired yet?"

In the '55 flood, he helped everyone raise docks by hand, secure boats, nearly three days' worth of scrambling and sleeplessness. And then? The hospital. Jim was fine, but his first daughter, Lynne, was on the way. Docks to hospital and back. Lynne's middle name became Diane, after one of the two hurricanes, along with Connie, that gathered together on weather maps like two fried eggs in a pan, dumping intense rain on the region.

On a sturdy tree in the lower Washington Crossing Park, Jim nailed a sign commemorating the water level, near the creek where we used to net fish, but they never seem to come in there anymore. The sign is down because the tree, an ash, is too. The ash trees once planted along this scenic byway, Route 29—a portion of which is named for Daniel Bray, who gathered the Durham boats used in the crossing—are being taken down as a result of the emerald ash borer. So, too, are the ash trees on the riverbank, and the one I used to stare into outside my bedroom window.

I walked a little on the towpath on my last night, regaining my land legs, and saw signs of newer infestations. Something called bacterial leaf scorch. I had a conversation on the Lenape trip with Frank, who wanted to "live and let live." But take that philosophy too far in this context and the non-native crowds out the native species. Frank, a fisherman, granted he did not want to catch a snakehead (nor have them crowd out the bass), and the spotted lanternfly from Asia was hurting a prized apple tree. It was hard not to think about how through a changing climate and the globalization that traffics invasive species, the human hand has blighted nearly every tree, creek, and stone.

In 1989, the year I graduated college, Joyce Carol Oates wrote an essay, "Against Nature," set on the towpath in Titusville. While riding her bike she had an attack of tachycardia and describes lying on her back on the dirt-gravel staring up at the sky. Lying prone, she contemplates nature, but also nature writing, which tends too easily toward "REVERENCE, AWE, PIETY, MYSTICAL ONENESS." She would prefer not *nature-in-itself* but *nature-as-experience*. In the former, nature is merely a collection of nouns, out there. In the latter, it is filtered through the senses, our expectations, stories. I am inclined to agree with her, and once or twice saw her riding that very towpath with her late husband trailing. However, there is something to be said for encountering nature on its own non-anthropocentric terms. It exists for more than our benefit. Yet she's right that it needs a story, and not just a romantic communion with.

These are limited responses, ones we have been so accustomed to see that they have become cliché. Nature is also randy and rowdy, full of ants, chiggers, ticks, and leeches. Nature is never static, but it's getting harder and harder to feel that transcendental "oneness" when so much is dying and disappearing. Now the more familiar responses might be indignation, abjection, grief, resignation with occasional but diminishing hope. But if we are to turn this battle around, we will still need beauty—a cause worth fighting for.

Walking through the park yesterday, I thought of it as a kind of palimpsest, a painting where an older painting shows through. Old restrooms still stood there, made from river stone, just a bench and a hole in the ground, and right beside them newer structures with modern conveniences. Old picnic tables hung on too, with concrete structures and thick, rotting planks right next to ones with metal frames and treated lumber. Old stone firepits resembling small hearths sit next to the picnic table, with new sturdy metal grills right beside. The faint remains of a former world still pressing into the now. The towpath, once a place for pulling barges, then a railroad, now a bike and walking path.

The bridge is built at the site of the old McKonkey Ferry, and on McKonkey Island there used to be fireworks on the Fourth of July. I used to love the celebration, people lining the bridge or anchoring their boats to watch the spectacle, the night sky illuminated in a crackle pattern, wait for the astonishing boom. Now that I'm older I get why they unnerve dogs—too much unnecessary violence, drama.

Washington crossed here on Christmas night, turning around a beleaguered army and a failing war effort. His army had suffered a series of defeats and strategic retreats, and supplies were badly depleted. Enlistments would expire on New Year's Eve, and many of the troops wanted to go home. Washington needed a win and secured it through stealth.

The existing ferries were key to the crossing. As much as Washington had to get his army across, he had to ferry the horses and cannons across too. For the men, he confiscated some Durham boats, fifty feet long, about eight feet wide, double-ended like a big canoe. The men might have hopped into these, but the horses and cannons required the flat-bottomed ferries. There's a reproduction of one at the landing site.

The Johnson House still stands on the New Jersey side, the only structure remaining from the day of the crossing, a 1740 farmhouse with a spring house. Here, Washington and his army regrouped. The original plan included two other crossings, one at the Trenton ferry and another at Bristol, but they were thwarted by ice. Washington began to despair of a surprise attack but was himself undeterred.

There's a statue reproduction of the iconic Emanuel Leutze painting in the park on the Pennsylvania side. In the painting the river is choked with ice, which it was, but the river is also a lot wider, more likely the painter's native Rhine than the Delaware. Also, the boat is too small for the dozen in it, perhaps to make George, standing, look even more heroic. The general ought to know we don't stand in small boats, right Sully? But the artist is painting steely determination, or the precarious nature of the early republic.

The men appear to be members of the local militia, and some were. Three men row at the bow of the boat. One is an African American, another wears the bonnet of a Scotsman, and the third a coonskin cap. Two farmers, in broad-brimmed hats, huddle against cold in the middle, while the man at the stern wears leggings, moccasins, and a shoulder pouch, and likely represents an Indigenous member of Washington's troop.

Hoff writes that when the first toll bridge was built here a "Quaker painter" executed two paintings of Washington and his "steed," nailing them to either end of the bridge. When the bridge was destroyed by a "freshet," one of them was taken by Landlord Jamison of Taylorsville (and subsequently the Historical Society of Pennsylvania), and "the other fell into the hands of the proprietor of the Washington's Crossing hotel." He says it adorns the bar of the "hostelrie" on the Jersey side, what used to be the Tally Ho Tavern, now Patriot's Crossing. If it's there, or at the Washington Crossing Inn, I have not seen it.

While Leutze captures some of the diversity of the "crossing" of frontier America, the painting has been reinterpreted numerous times, most recently by Kent Monkman, *Resurgence of the People* (2019). The Met, which also houses the Leutze, placed Monkman's painting (nearly the same sprawling size) even more prominently than the original—in the Great Hall. Monkman inserts a number of Indigenous people and refugees and replaces Washington with Miss Chief Eagle Testickle (you read that right), an Indigenous, gender-fluid mythological hero. A modern-day "militia" looks on from the distance, guns raised high. Two in the boat (Black) pull those struggling in the water (white) back in, ferry them across. A man in a tie seems to fight the progress, so he is kept out.

Washington hoped to cross by midnight but landed closer to three in the morning, the entire crossing of the army taking about nine hours.

Then they reconnoitered, walked east up the hill, took a right at what is now Bear Tavern Road, pulled the horses and cannons across Jacob's Creek, surprised some mercenary Hessians, and changed the course of history.

My stepfather, Tim West, discovered through genealogical research that he is a descendent of a crosser, Josiah Hand. That earned him a spot in the boat in the reenactment on Christmas Day. And he has since worked with the Friends of Washington Crossing State Park to help tell the story of what happened here. He and my mother went to high school together, to some dances together, reconnected years later, married.

I passed under the bridge, crawling with morning commuters. Built in 1904 on the original 1831 masonry piers, its narrow borders slow you down, squeeze the traffic through, often popping off mirrors. People race to get across before other cars encroach, as if exhaling then holding their breath.

Past the bridge, I sipped my coffee. My mother was still in good health but starting to decline. At breakfast that morning, on the walk the evening before, she showed some signs that her gait had stiffened, mobility slowed (Parkinson's we would later learn), although she still finished the cross-word before me. She still knows the birthdays of her children, grandchildren, friends, their children, co-workers, neighbors, the mailman. She has a head for numbers, sure—she was a math teacher after all—but it's a sign of her showing care. In conversations among my sisters, she remembers how old we were at family vacations, our camping in the Keys, rock-hopping in Acadia, the run down Sleeping Bear Dunes. At our recent family reunions, when we have overloaded her house and kitchen (and septic), her ability to tend to the needs of her nine grandchildren, make the dips and salads, supervise the grilling, greet old friends, had been curtailed. She wanted to sit, find stillness, watch the melee from the comfort of a porch chair, one she could get out of. Her father died when she was three, her twin sisters two months old. An engineer, he came home from World War II, where he commanded a Black battalion (the 530th Quartermaster) to supervise a highway crew. Though he survived D-Day and the Battle of the Bulge, he was struck by a car four months after being discharged. My grandmother knew that you are not your circumstances. That you are what you make of them. She kept at it, carried on, persevered, passed on those qualities to her daughter.

I began to think of the inevitable, of the short time we have together, and pictured myself trying to say something at her funeral. When I said I wanted to go to school out West, *go where you want.* When I said I was changing from premed to English, *you can major in what you want.* I saw my daughter reading something I wrote in my place, because I probably wouldn't be able, and then something very unexpected, something very different from the laughter and lightness just an hour before, tears welling from the inside.

I had to put the paddle down, rest it across the gunwales of the canoe. The shaft was light ash with brown walnut stripes inlaid in the blade, a black rock guard at the tip, and a T-grip at the top. Get a grip. I let the river spin me.

Then I did what I had been doing for the past 195 miles. I put blade in water and pulled. The water created a small vortex I stared into. The bow lifted some, and I was moving again. I paddled toward a small family of mergansers, a momma of five, and they let me get closer than they ever had the whole trip.

They reminded me that the very impulse to grieve was entwined with joy; that stitched somewhere in sadness was a thread of happiness. Throughout the trip, I had been alternately cheerful and sullen, sunbaked and waterlogged, but I just kept on, borne by the river.

I glided on toward Scudders Falls. Amos Scudder was a local militia-man who participated in the march to Trenton, although the falls bear the name of another Scudder who died here in 1754. An old wing dam creates what Hoff calls a "drop and rough race." The water sluices through a chute, picks up velocity, tumbles into waves. Letcher says it is very popular with the Mohawk Canoe Club of Trenton, around since 1903. My grandfather was a member.

At the base, I caught an eddy, and parked on a gravelly island. Someone had placed two chairs there, along with a grill on the firepit, and tied a piece of driftwood to a rope hung from a tree, making a swing. Huck would be at home here. I would too. And all in the shadow of I-95, the main north-south highway connecting Eastern seaports, a megalopolis sometimes called BosWash. On a pole there appeared to be something like an osprey igloo.

The island is called Blackguard, as in a rude or dishonorable man, one who swears. An 1873 annual report prepared by the chief of engineers, Clarence King, refers to the island as "a favored resort of indigent gentle-men of leisure."

Writer Dan Aubrey found that the island is privately owned, going back to 1928, and currently on the city of Trenton's tax records. James Capasso, of the Trenton Division of Economic Development, told Au-brey that "the owner is current on taxes which are about $1,000 per year total." It is assessed at $16,600, which would put the value at $20,000, "although you would probably have a hard time doing an accurate ap-praisal given few or no comparable sales."

Below that, Yardley boat ramp, a common place to take out. Once when working my summer job, canoe and tube transport, the truck got stuck. I got out to push, the driver gunned it before I was ready, and a large grapefruit-sized rock flew into my middle. I doubled over in pain, saw a scrape down there, worried I would never have children, or speak again. Near here, on the other side, my parents would come, and theirs, before any boats or docks. Not unlike the merry ten in Frenchtown.

My mother's maternal grandfather, Harry McLean, was born in England. He apprenticed as a baker when about ten, came to America around 1909, because people in his community came. Mostly potters from Stoke-on-Trent, they settled in Prospect Heights, because the area had a similar clay soil good for pottery. Harry McLean established a bakery.

Trenton once led the nation in pottery. Lenox made fine china here and Maddock Pottery later became American Standard, your fine porcelain.

Her paternal grandfather, Gustave Meury, came from Switzerland to be a brewmaster at what was called the People's Brewing Company. They made Trenton Old Stock until prohibition. The same factory—which overlooked the river—would later produce the famous (or infamous) Pink Champale. The brewery was owned by the Kuser family who built an estate on Baldpate Mountain, above Titusville and the river.

Time unfurled before me, a tale of rivers formed and canals made, towns rising and trees growing, creatures being born and dying, struggle and harmony, betrayal and mercy, season following season time and again like a waterwheel, a paddle. For all our gauges and topographic maps, our measuring of cubic feet per second, the river is hard to contain. Despite all we have thrown at it, the river endures our attempts to dam and impair, impede, and pollute. Like the body, it carries on.

One thing about a river is that it flows through your consciousness as it flows on its course. Problems begin to fade and serenity increases without the ceaseless flow of interruptions, obligations. The river becomes time, the current keeps it, merging into impression and memory. The river smooths out obstacles, unties knots, scatters anxieties, recreates the spirit.

Our lives are as rivers. They contain long mundane stretches punctuated by occasional heart-pounding rapids. They have falls—abrupt changes in direction or flow—and compelling eddy pauses, with sporadic, isolating periods of drought or duress, when fish (or the flesh) weaken. They carry all they can, coursing and pulsing with the life within, going where they must.

≈ ≈ ≈

In 1886, John Boyle O'Reilly wrote in the *Boston Pilot* of his trip on the Delaware that he had "seen the land truly, with its wealth and strength, who has followed the rivers from their sources in the hills down to the tide-pulsating ocean-heart." He salutes the Delaware with "love and admiration." Among the other rivers he canoed—the Connecticut, Susquehanna, Merrimack—"on our list of canoeing-rivers we must give the first place to the Delaware."

Within ten minutes of setting out from Port Jervis, O'Reilly described the sensations he experienced:

> To plunge the bare arms to the elbow into the river as you go, and let the cool water curl up to the biceps; to feel the soft breeze on bare head and neck; to be far from the busy crowds in the cities, with all the senses awake to new and fascinating objects—the swirl of rapid water, the brown and yellow stones on the bottom of the river, the large, free movements of clouds, the strange flowers on the bank; to grip the paddle with an agreeable sense of power in shoulder and hand; to brace the feet strongly against the footrest and feel the canoe spring with the elastic force of the stroke; to shout unrestrainedly to your companions, and hear them shout in return like hearty, natural men; to laugh consumedly with slight cause; and in the midst of all this joyous wakefulness, to be aware of the nearing rapid ahead—to hear its low, steady roar, as if the sound clung to the water; and to be aware also of a new preparation of nerve, sight, and muscle—a purely animal and instinctive alertness—for the moment of rushing excitement into which you are sweeping.

Boyle noted that they were all silent at first and surprised. "It took us some moments to realize that the surprise was delight." Hoff wrote that each person on his trip read O'Reilly's account. This and "other works gave occasion to frequent references to the gentlemanly advocate of out-of-door culture." Their thoughts and craft "were running in the same channels." O'Reilly died in 1890 at age forty-six, causing Hoff to reflect: "In common with thousands of others, Trenton canoemen heard with deep sorrow the story of his end, the testimony from all that at the close as in the nigh noon of his life he was truly noble."

I passed under the multiple-arch bridge carrying SEPTA trains from Philadelphia to West Trenton. At the end of the line, I remembered an old tavern, Freddie's, near my grandmother's house, where we used to eat.

Then I came to Rotary Island, where Hoff and crew landed, had their Park Island club. With him on that trip was Fred Donnelly, who would

serve as mayor of Trenton (1911–1932). By about 1908 they began looking for another use for the island. William B. Maddock, of the pottery
Maddocks, secretary of the canoe club and a leading Rotarian, helped
with the land transfer in 1918. He, Donnelly, and others had the idea to
use the island as a health retreat for children affected by tuberculosis and
poor air quality. The Mercer County Tuberculosis and Sanitation League,
which Donnelly served as president, would send children for two weeks
of regulated camp life on the island. They aimed to fight tuberculosis with
fresh air, sunlight, wholesome diet, exercise, and rest, much like the sanitariums upriver near Narrowsburg. The Rotary Club sold the island in
1966. It is now owned by Washington Crossing State Park though not
managed in any particular way and vulnerable to flooding.

Because of our own recent immersion in the plague, it might be easier
to understand how much the fatality of illness affected our immediate
ancestors.

At the tip of the island, I could just make out the gold leaf–covered
dome of the New Jersey State Capitol Building and the "Trenton Makes"
bridge. On the bridge are the words "TRENTON MAKES THE WORLD
TAKES." Once in a pensive mood I traveled across the river by train, and
the *m* was either not lit or blocked by the window frame, so it looked like
Trenton "akes" (in the other window, "THE WORLD TAKES," which
could also take on meaning). At the Dingman's Ferry boat ramp, the filmmaker Sonia Szczesna and I had briefly talked about why Trenton had not
undergone, as of yet, a revitalization as was happening in other postindus-
trial cities. Perhaps Rotary Island could be like Belle Isle in Richmond, an
accessible city park? One thing they had tried was to build a minor league
baseball stadium. My father was director of the Mercer County Improvement Authority when it was constructed, so his name is on the plaque. We
once caught Derek Jeter on a rehab assignment when the Thunder was a
Yankees farm team. Coincidentally, every major and minor league baseball team uses a mud found in a tributary of the river just south of here to
de-gloss, and maybe bless new baseballs.

The story we tell about a place, or a person, or an event, is important to
any revitalization. "All sorrows can be borne if you put them into a story
or tell a story about them," Isak Dinesen has been quoted as saying. Loss
can be deeply felt, but stories help recover, renew.

The Old Barracks, which housed the British in the French and Indian War, was a hospital during the Revolutionary, are up there, as is the state museum, which displays a Lenape dugout canoe made from a hollowed-out poplar, found in the mud in the 1860s. I visited it on school field trips. It measures fourteen feet long and about a foot and a half wide—not far off solo canoes we still paddle today (near identical to Hoff's). The Lenape name for the tulip tree is *muxulhemenshi*, "tree from which canoes are made."

≈ ≈ ≈

Looking at the bridge from the island, I realized too late I should have kept going under the bridge to meet the tidewater.

As I paddled into the final cove, our agreed pick-up site, a light wind picked up, caught me enough so that I couldn't steer in. Again, as at Snuffy's, it's as if something is preventing me from finishing. I have felt a sense of purpose in the rhythm of the river, one I am not ready to let go of. In a few days there will be meetings, and university politics, and the latest burdens we will carry from the news. What the river gave most was a sense of calm, often a little more chill than the air. How to carry it forward? I want to take a part of it with me. The heart is a little sore, not wanting to leave what for nine days has been home. Coming out of the river is harder than going in.

I could text or call, say pick me up below the bridge at the marine terminal, but that would complicate things, cause undue worry. I look back at the island and almost can't believe what I see perched high in the bare-limbed crown of a tree. Yet another eagle, as if it has been marking my progress all along, or telling me not to leave. Not wanting any of it to end, eagle sightings, summer, is a sure sign of living.

When it comes to regret, I am thinking it is best to pack light. One great thing about a river is that it really doesn't know reverse. In the end, a river will do what it does. Say what it has to say. Argue for itself and its own power. Mostly you have to follow it. You can choose to go around this rock or that island, but for the most part you make your best guess and paddle on.

On the river, you learn to accept what the river wants, to take what it gives. You submit to it. And you can substitute other words here, like "reality," or the "universe." "In a life properly lived," the poet and novelist Jim Harrison once told the *Paris Review*, "you're a river. You touch things lightly or deeply; you move along because life herself moves, and you can't stop it."

After my stroke, my mind kept returning to where my life had run aground, what had led me to try to fight the current. After my separation from my wife, some of the same patterns, searching for clues, wanting answers. Every time you capsize, you learn. But looking back, I could see no simple answers, no hidden rocks below the surface. I had to remain open to uncertainty. And to live in what was given. When I was able to do that, I could see the miracle in the ordinary, the wonder in the everyday.

Ruth Jones remembered every spill, but I have been trying to focus on the triumphs of the past two hundred miles, the past twenty years. The fall two years ago—to the day—was a kind of crucible, a kiln in a factory to cast something new. A fresh clean porcelain plate like the kind they used to make right here.

The same year Hoff wrote his book on the Delaware cruise, 1892, a Swiss geologist, Albert Heim, delivered a paper to the Swiss Alpine Club, "The Experience of Dying from Falls." Heim was leading a party down a steep snowfield when he lost his footing and slid over a precipice. During a fall of over sixty feet, his thoughts were coherent and clear, and time slowed to a crawl: "what I felt in five to ten seconds could not be described in ten times that length of time." After his impact, Heim remained unconscious for half an hour. His companions carried him down to the nearest alpine hut. When he came to, he eventually reflected on the event:

> I considered how the news of my death would arrive for my loved ones and
> I consoled them in my thoughts. Then I saw my whole past life take place
> in many images, as though on a stage at some distance from me. I saw my-
> self as the chief character in the performance. Everything was transfigured
> as though by a heavenly light and everything was beautiful without grief,
> without anxiety, and without pain. The memory of very tragic experiences
> I had had was clear but not saddening. I felt no conflict or strife; conflict
> had been transmuted into love. Elevated and harmonious thoughts domi-
> nated and united the individual images, and like magnificent music a divine

calm swept through my soul. I became ever more surrounded by a splendid blue heaven with delicate roseate and violet cloudlets. I swept into it painlessly and softly and I saw that now I was falling freely through the air and that under me a snow field lay waiting. Objective observations, thoughts, and subjective feelings were simultaneous. Then I heard a dull thud and my fall was over.

In addition to studying geology, Heim decided to make a study of the phenomenon. In a mountaineering fall, or similar accident, what did the victim experience in the last seconds of his life? He collected the stories of others and found that in practically all individuals who faced death through accidental falls, a similar mental state developed:

> There was no anxiety, no trace of despair, no pain; but rather calm seriousness, profound acceptance, and a dominant mental quickness and sense of surety. Mental activity became enormous, rising to a hundred-fold velocity or intensity. . . . In many cases there followed a sudden review of the individual's entire past; and finally the person falling often heard beautiful music and fell in a superbly blue heaven containing roseate cloudlets. Then consciousness was painlessly extinguished, usually at the moment of impact, and the impact was, at the most, heard but never painfully felt.

Heim, a talented artist and writer in addition to a scientist, inclines toward mysticism. Heim's paper was eventually translated into English and published in a 1972 edition of the journal *Omega*, dedicated to "the psychological study of dying, death, bereavement, suicide and other lethal behaviors" by Russell Noyes Jr., a psychiatrist at the University of Iowa, and Roy Kletti. Noyes compared Heim's findings with more recent crisis experiences that he had collected himself, such as that of a young man who was traveling in a car going sixty miles an hour when the steering failed, and who reported that his "mind was working rapidly and reviewed information from driver's education that might bear on what I should do to save myself."

Serious research followed Noyes's work, and in 1975 Raymond Moody published the best-selling *Life after Life*, which established the term "near-death experience," moving the science into the realm of the paranormal. Rare liminal moments of mortal danger that occurred in the lives of healthy people were also linked with sick people in hospitals who died on the operating table and came back to life.

The *Handbook of Near-Death Experiences* summarizes the common themes Moody and others observed in many NDEs:

> Feelings of peace and quiet; hearing noises such as buzzing and windlike sounds; a sensation of being out of the body; passing through a tunnel; meeting other individuals such as deceased friends; encountering a being of light; having a life review; reaching a border that, if crossed, meant the NDErs could not return to life; and finding that they had returned to their physical bodies.

I saw no "roseate clouds" like Heim, but I was in them when in the helicopter, rising up over the mountains, lifting me skyward. There were buzzing and wind-like sounds but those were likely the whirling blades and motion through the sky. A panoramic view—I had a partial one of the mountains, as much as I could see out, and some sense of things unfinished, like Heim. He wanted to give his lecture in five days, and I had classes to teach in four. No tunnel, no light, but I did experience the sense of calm Heim describes, the "profound acceptance." Some overriding sense it would all somehow be okay. And when I came to in the hospital room, gratitude for all in the room, and to be alive.

Any brush with mortality teaches compassion. It grants forbearance on personal failings, perspective on partisan divisions, patience with the suffering of others. It teaches the strength born in community rather than in individual striving.

The last night of the trip, in our family home, I looked in the mirror for the first time in a long while. Had I changed? There had been some erosion over the years, like on islands, but also accretion too, if not in paddle-arm strength, experiences. While recovering the previous year, I had read that only 10 percent of stroke victims recover completely and that 40 percent are significantly impaired. Hardly a day goes by that I don't realize that I'm on borrowed time. Indeed, we all make assumptions about time and age, but the answer may be quite simple. We have today. A place to start and end and a good deal to savor in between.

I came to the river because it was the place I was born, like some anadromous homing fish. I was born from water too, am mostly made of the stuff—we all are. We are christened with it, washed clean by it. When I die, sprinkle some of my ashes right here in it.

Thinking of Harry McLean had me thinking of Norman Maclean (no relation), who wrote *A River Runs through It*. The title comes from the last few lines, about how "eventually, all things merge into one, and a river runs through it." But I've always wondered about that vague "it." The river runs through the merging oneness? It's a metaphor, I know, but might it be more apt to say a river runs through us? We feel its motion, its connection, its pull. We pulse with it, feel its power, and are moved by it. We want to join, as it does, with the wider world, here just below the fall line. When the water reaches the ocean, it evaporates into clouds and cycles back to the headwaters.

I thought back to Sherri's question from the first day of my solo trip. Was I going through something? I answered flippantly that we all were, but we all really were. I met people who had gone through heart surgery, hip surgery, connective tissue disease, rehab, a throat stabbing, crack addiction, nicotine addiction, confidence deficits, OCD, depression, divorce. Stasis was abnormal. We were all moving, transitioning.

I started north in higher elevation, traveling down and south, river-borne, but it also seemed I was traveling up, rising.

Was I going through something? Yes, I was going through a river, and it was going through me. I was going through trees, by some islands, often a canyon with high bluffs, through these historic towns, under the bridges that tied them together. I was trying to find the right channel, read the water, find a clean line through.

And to answer a question I started with, *why the river?* I know for me it's the hypnotic flow of it, the life within it, the vibrancy and force. For others, there are so many reasons that I have seen up and down the river. We come to the river to remember, we come to forget. We come for fun, for family, to recreate, to experience, explore, to teach kids, to learn history, to reenact it. Shall we gather at the river? Indeed we shall. We shall come to eat, to pray, to drink, swim, read, dive, snorkel, wade, to dare to jump from on high, camp, fish, to join with friends and with family, to make friends, watch birds, look for treasures or artifacts, to make love, play music, cool down, trip, heal from sickness, to enjoy ourselves. A river binds us to people and to all the creatures who share it.

Up on shore, waiting for my shuttle, sitting cross-legged, I had the sensation I was still on the water, river lapping at my side. The boat glides lightly on the water, through the coming waves. The next stroke pulls me closer, and the next.

Lower Trenton Bridge, Bridge Street Bridge, or "Trenton Makes" Bridge, 1928.

FERRIES (ACKNOWLEDGMENTS)

Ferries help you cross the river from one place to the other. My warm thanks to Gary Letcher for talking with me pre-trip and for his book on the river, an invaluable guide. Thanks to Rick Lander and Ruth Jones for speaking with me as well. To Ruth especially for all her work on behalf of the river. I am grateful to Kathleen Sandt for putting me in touch with Ruth and for answering other questions about the National Park Service, and thanks to her daughter Calla for the video on Ruth. Thanks Kate Schmidt and John Yagecic with the DRBC for talking water quality and to Maya K. van Rossum for all you do on behalf of the river. Thanks to the many people I spoke with on the bank or in their boats, like Andrea Conner and brother Scott Arnold. Danielle McDowell at the diner—your journey is harder than mine and thanks for the ride. Special thanks to the Equinunk five and the Frenchtown ten for the hospitality and acquaintance.

Thanks so much to Dave Simon for sharing his stories and to wife Jane and the rest of the safety crew—Jacqui, Sherri, Wes, Louise—for guiding us safely down. Thanks Adam DePaul for coordinating the trip and Shelley DePaul for all she does for the Lenape Nation. Thanks Chief Chuck for the ride and for some laughs. Thanks to T. Storm Heter for the philosophical asides on and off the water. Thanks to all on the 2022 journey for being so welcoming—*wanishi* twelve times in the smoke of cedar-sage.

Many thanks to librarians for help, including Alyssa Archer at Radford and Kathy McGuire in Trenton. Don Hamilton, Diane Rosencrance, and Tom Wittig did their best to answer eagle questions.

Thanks to the English teacher who told the class I would be a writer.

Thanks to many neighbors in Titusville: Roger Miller for use of the dock and steps, Bill Cane (and Patrick and Michael) for the boat rides up, Bob Burd for keeping up with the dock when he could, Judy Abbott Neiderer for keeping her father's river spirit alive.

Thanks Elliot and Catherine for making the call. Thank you first responders, helicopter pilot, doctors in Roanoke.

Tim Poland and Dan Woods offered hilarity, humor, and a hospital visit. Tim puts up with (points out) my typos. Paul Bogard and Susan Fox Rogers offered valuable insight, valuable models of good writing. John Lane encouraged a book on the Delaware, cheers river writers everywhere. Thanks my fellow Mercer County native John McPhee for his many books on rocks and rivers and for almost blurbing.

Gordie Thompson provided the map. Thanks Michael McGandy for expressing interest and Mahinder Kingra for pushing the craft along. Marlyn Miller smoothed out the dings and scratches and Susan Specter pointed out potential hazards. Thanks to Cornell and Three Hills staff. More books, please.

Thanks to any and all paddle partners—Bob Barnes, Josh Carroll, Ralph Robertson, Rick Roth, Sam Van Noy. Tracey and Fred Abell on the Middle Fork and Deschutes. Thorpe Moeckel writes about rivers as well as he paddles them.

Special thanks to my shuttle mom and ground crew Tim West. And warm appreciation and heartfelt gratitude to Brit Washburn for encouraging me on the river and back into the river of words.

MAPS (BIBLIOGRAPHY)

My main guides on the river were J. Wallace Hoff and Gary Letcher. Hoff is quoted from a printed facsimile of his 1893 edition. A free and searchable one is available through the Library of Congress. Letcher provides mile-by-mile description, so any quoted material should be easy to track. For texts not so extensively quoted and where possible, page numbers are provided after references below. I often used other online texts or replicas, as in the case of John Boyle O'Reilly, whose *Boston Pilot* article was reprinted in *Athletics and Manly Sport*. Most sources from newspapers and journals came from online versions. "Pleasantest river" comes from van der Donck and not Hudson, as it is often attributed. His *Representation of New Netherland* (1650) seems a rough draft of the later *Description of New Netherland* (1655). Burroughs's "A Summer Voyage" can be found in *Pepacton*.

I did not list certain well-known texts, such as the *Adventures of Huckleberry Finn*, *Moby Dick*, or *Walden*—any good edition will do. Twain's quote about "drifting down the big still river," comes from early in chapter 12. Melville's "cipher" is from chapter 99, "The Doubloon," and Thoreau's thoughts on a "perpetual morning," his bragging like chanticleer, are in chapter 2, "Where I Lived." The chanticleer quote was the book's epigraph when printed in 1854 and was conceived on a boating trip in the early fog on the Sudbury and Assabet Rivers (see Thorson, p. 7). My epigraph is from a manuscript in the Berg Collection of the New York Public Library and is quoted in Thorson, p. 5. Freud's thoughts on the big questions concerning eel reproductive organs come from Svensson, p. 46. Johannes Schmidt's pursuit of the eel comes from *The Book of Eels* as well, p. 75. Isak Dinesen is quoted in Arendt.

≈ ≈ ≈

Abbey, Edward. *Desert Solitaire: A Season in the Wilderness.* New York: Simon and Schuster, 1968. Reprint, New York: Touchstone, 1990, 152, 165.

Abbey, Edward. "Down the River with Henry David Thoreau." In *The Best of Edward Abbey*, 272–307. San Francisco: Sierra Club, 1984, 279, 295, 307.

Albert, Richard. *Damming the Delaware: The Rise and Fall of Tocks Island Dam.* University Park: Pennsylvania State University Press, 1987, 136.

Angell, Roger. *This Old Man: All in Pieces.* New York: Anchor, 2016, 281.

Arendt, Hannah. *The Human Condition.* Chicago: University of Chicago Press, 1958, 175.

Aubrey, Dan. "Discovery on the Delaware: Exploring the Famous River's Forgotten Islands." *CommunityNews.org*, July 28, 2017; updated January 11, 2022. https://www.communitynews.org/towns/ewing-observer/discovery-on-the-delaware-exploring-the-famous-river-s-forgotten-islands/article_c45879fd-0edd-54a6-99f9-6c85e-ba2e540.html.

Bowler, Kate. *Everything Happens for a Reason: And Other Lies I've Loved.* New York: Random House, 2018.

Burroughs, John. "A Critical Glance into Thoreau." *Atlantic Monthly*, June 1919.

Burroughs, John. *Far and Near.* Boston: Houghton Mifflin, 1904, 133.

Burroughs, John. *Pepacton.* Boston: Houghton Mifflin, 1881, 7–48.

Carson, Rachel. *Under the Sea-Wind: A Naturalist's Picture of Ocean Life.* New York: Simon and Schuster, 1941. Reprint, New York: Oxford University Press, 1952, 221, 254, 260.

Cusk, Rachel. *Coventry.* New York: Farrar, Straus and Giroux, 2019, 226.

Dale, Frank. *Delaware Diary: Episodes in the Life of a River.* New Brunswick, NJ: Rutgers University Press, 1996, 29.

Deloria, Philip J. *Playing Indian.* New Haven: Yale University Press, 1998, 126.

Descriptive Pamphlet for the Loomis Sanatorium for the Treatment of Tuberculosis. Liberty, NY: Loomis Sanitorium, 1903. https://collections.nlm.nih.gov/bookviewer?PID=nlm:nlmuid-101174114-bk.

Donahue, John. "Debunking Myths about Delaware Water Gap Getting a National Park Designation." *Lehigh ValleyLive.com*. March 7, 2022. https://www.lehighvalleylive.com/opinion/2022/03/debunking-myths-about-delaware-water-gap-getting-a-national-park-designation-opinion.html.

Douglas, William O. "The Public Be Dammed." *Playboy* 17, no. 7, July 1969, 143–82.

Dunn, Stephen. *Falling Backwards into the World: 20 Short Poems*. New York: Jane Street Press, 2012, 14.

"Famous River Hot Dog Man Greg Crance, Who Fed Thousands on the Delaware River, Dies at 56." *Philadelphia Inquirer*. May 13, 2021.

Figura, David. "One Man's Solitary Life of Trapping, Smoking and Selling Eels on the Delaware River." *New York Upstate*. August 29, 2021.

Gallagher, Sarah H. *1703–1903: Early History of Lambertville*. Trenton, NJ: MacCrellish & Quigley, 1903, 37–38.

Gilbert, Elizabeth. *Eat, Pray, Love: One Woman's Search for Everything across Italy, India, and Indonesia*. New York: Riverhead, 2006.

Graves, John. *Goodbye to a River: A Narrative*. New York: Knopf, 1959. Reprint, New York: Vintage, 2002, 4, 292.

Griffiths, R. R, W. A. Richards, U. McCann, and R. Jesse. "Psilocybin Can Occasion Mystical-Type Experiences Having Substantial and Sustained Personal Meaning and Spiritual Significance." *Psychopharmacology*. 2006. https://www.hopkinsmedicine.org/press_releases/2006/griffithspsilocybin.pdf.

Grumet, Robert S. "The Selling of Lenapehoking." *Bulletin of the Archaeological Society of New Jersey* 44 (1989): 1–5.

Francis, Maria, and Kathryne Rubright. "Shawnee on Delaware Flooding after Nor'easter Pours Rain on River Basin." *Pocono Record*, October 27, 2021.

Harris, Eddy L. *Mississippi Solo: A River Quest*. New York: Holt, 1988, 13, 68.

Harrison, Jim. "The Art of Fiction, No. 104." Interview by Jim Fergus. *The Paris Review* 107 (Summer 1988).

Hoff, J. Wallace. Obituary. "Funeral Saturday for Fire Official." *Trenton Evening Times*, December 13, 1922.

Hoff, J. Wallace. *Two Hundred Miles on the Delaware River: A Canoe Cruise from Its Headwaters to the Falls of Trenton*. Trenton, NJ: Brandt, 1893.

"Hoffs Like Titusville." *Trenton Evening Times*. June 10, 1904.

Holden, Janice Miner, Bruce Greyson, and Debbie James. *The Handbook of Near-Death Experiences: Thirty Years of Investigation*. Westport, CT: Praeger, 2009, 18.

Holling, Holling Clancy. *Paddle-to-the-Sea*. New York: Houghton Mifflin, 1941.

Johnson, Ayanna Elizabeth, and Katherine K. Wilkinson, eds. *All We Can Save: Truth, Courage, and Solutions for the Climate Crisis*. New York: One World, 2021, xxii–xxiv.

King, Clarence. *Report of the Chief of Engineers: Survey of the Delaware River between Trenton, New Jersey, and Easton, Pennsylvania*. Washington, DC: Government Printing Office, 1873, 916.

Lane, John. *My Paddle to the Sea: Eleven Days on the River of the Carolinas*. Athens: University of Georgia Press, 2011.

Lembke, Anna. *Dopamine Nation: Finding Balance in the Age of Indulgence*. New York: Penguin, 2021.

Letcher, Gary. *Canoeing the Delaware River: A Guide to the River and Shore*. New Brunswick, NJ: Rutgers University Press, 1985.

Lopez, Barry. *River Notes: The Dance of Herons*. New York: Avon, 1979, 81, 26.

Maclean, Norman. *A River Runs through It*. Chicago: University of Chicago Press, 1989.

Markhem, James M. "Tocks Island: Home to Squatters." *New York Times*, September 8, 1971.

Matthiessen, Peter. *The Snow Leopard*. New York: Penguin, 1978, 249.

McPhee, John. *Annals of the Former World*. New York: Farrar, Straus and Giroux, 1998, 182–83.

McPhee, John. *The Founding Fish*. New York: Farrar, Straus and Giroux, 2002, 214, 351.

Moody, Raymond A., Jr. *Life after Life*. New York: Mockingbird Books, 1975, 18.

Muir, John. *The Yosemite*. New York: The Century Co., 1912, 262.

"'My Work is Never Done': The Lasting Legacy of Nancy Shukaitis and Her Fight against the Tocks Island Dam." *Morning Call*. March 22, 2021.

Ney, Joel. "K. K. Kuzminsky, Iconic Cultural Patriarch of the Soviet Émigré Community, Has Died." *Art Daily*. August 31, 2023. https://artdaily.cc/news/79742/K--K--Kuzminsky--iconic-cultural-patriarch-of-the-Soviet--migr--community--has-died.

Nobel, Justin. "The Miseducation of John Muir." *Atlas Obscura*. July 26, 2016.

Noyes, Russell, and Roy Kletti. "The Experience of Dying from Falls." Translated from Albert Heim. *Omega: The Journal of Death and Dying* 3, no. 1 (1972): 45–52, 50, 47.

Oates, Joyce Carol. "Against Nature." In *(Woman) Writer: Occasions and Opportunities*, 66–78. New York: Dutton, 1988.

O'Reilly, John Boyle. "Down the Delaware River in a Canoe." In *Athletics and Manly Sport*, 303–50. Boston: Pilot Publishing Company, 1890. Reprint, 1896.

"A Paddler's Dictionary." *Canoe and Kayak Magazine*. May 23, 2011.

Pinchot, Gifford. *Breaking New Ground*. New York: Harcourt, 1947. Reprint, Island Press, 1998, 505.

Pollan, Michael. *How to Change Your Mind: What the New Science of Psychedelics Teaches Us about Consciousness, Dying, Addiction, Depression, and Transcendence*. New York: Penguin, 2018, 390.

Powell, John Wesley. *The Exploration of the Colorado River and Its Canyons*. Meadville, PA: Flood & Vincent, 1895. Reprint, Dover, 1961, 212.

Privitar, Ginny. "Tom Quick: First Came the Legend, Then the Propaganda." *Pike County Courier*, May 23, 2014.

Prosek, James. "A Solitary Life Centered on Trapping River Eels." *New York Times*, August 19, 2006.

Purdy, Jedidiah. "Environmentalism's Racist History." *New Yorker*, August 13, 2015.

Rilke, Rainer Maria. *Book of Hours: Love Poems to God*. Translated by Joanna Macy and Anita Barrows. New York: Riverhead, 1997, 88.

Roche, James Jeffrey. *Life of John Boyle O'Reilly*. New York: Cassell, 1891.

Schutt, Amy C. *Peoples of the River Valleys: The Odyssey of the Delaware Indians*. Philadelphia: University of Pennsylvania Press, 2007.

Shafer, Mary. *Devastation on the Delaware: Stories and Images of the Deadly Flood of 1955*. Riegelsville, PA: Word Forge, 2005.

Shukaitis, Nancy. *Lasting Legacies of the Lower Minisink*. Self-published, 2007.

Soderlund, Jean R. *Lenape Country: Delaware Valley Society before William Penn*. Philadelphia: University of Pennsylvania Press, 2015.

Spengler, Samantha. "The First Philadelphians." *Philadelphia Magazine*, November 2021.

Steinberg, Ted. *Gotham Unbound: The Ecological History of Greater New York*. New York: Simon and Schuster, 2014, 9.

Strayed, Cheryl. *Wild: From Lost to Found on the Pacific Crest Trail*. New York, Vintage, 2012.

Svensson, Patrik. *The Book of Eels: Our Enduring Fascination with the Most Mysterious Creature in the Natural World*. New York: HarperCollins, 2020.

Thoreau, Henry David. *The Journal, 1837–1861*. New York: New York Review of Books, 2009.

Thoreau, Henry David. *A Week on the Concord and Merrimack Rivers*. Orleans, MA: Parnassus, 1987. First published 1849.

Thorson, Robert M. *The Boatman: Henry David Thoreau's River Years*. Cambridge, MA: Harvard University Press, 2017.

Thorson, Robert M. "Thoreau a 'Man of the River.'" Interview with Alex Ashlock on *Here and Now*, WBUR. May 16, 2017. https://www.wbur.org/hereandnow/2017/05/16/henry-david-thoreau-concord-river.

"Treaty of Renewed Friendship." Lenape Nation of Pennsylvania. https://www.lenapenation.org/1st-project.

United States Senate Subcommittee on Water Resources. *Tocks Island Deauthorization: Hearings before the Subcommittee on Water Resources of the Committee on Public Works*. United States Senate, 94th Congress, Second Session. Washington, DC: U.S. Government Printing Office, 1976, 345.

Van der Donck, Adriaen. *A Description of New Netherland*. Edited by Charles T. Gehring and William A. Starna. Translated by Diederik Willem Goedhuys. Lincoln: University of Nebraska Press, 2008, 74.

Van der Donck, Adriaen. *The Representation of New Netherlands, 1650*. In *Narratives of New Netherland, 1609–1664*. Edited by J. Franklin Jameson. Original Narratives of Early American History. New York: Charles Scribner's Sons, 1909, 313.

Wallace, David Foster. *This Is Water: Some Thoughts, Delivered on a Significant Occasion, about Living a Compassionate Life*. New York: Little, Brown, 2009, 77.

Walls, Laura Dassow. *Henry David Thoreau: A Life*. Chicago: University of Chicago Press, 2017, 134.

Wildes, Harry Emerson. *The Delaware*. Library of Congress Rivers of America Collection. New York: Farrar and Rinehart, 1940.

Williams, Florence. *Heartbreak: A Personal and Scientific Journey*. New York: W. W. Norton, 2022, 208.

Williams, William Carlos. *A Book of Poems: Al Que Quiere!* Boston: Four Seas, 1917, 43.